MORTAL VISION

THE WISDOM OF EURIPIDES

MORTAL VISION

THE WISDOM OF EURIPIDES

Robert Emmet Meagher

St. Martin's Press   New York

First published in the United States of America in 1989

Printed in the United States of America

ISBN 0-312-02720-6

Library of Congress Cataloging-in-Publication Data

Meagher, Robert E.
Mortal Vision : the wisdom of Euripedes / Robert Emmet Meagher.
p. cm.
Bibliography: p.
ISBN 0-312-02720-6
1. Euripedes--Criticism and interpretation. I Title.
PA3978.M39 1989
  882'.01--dc19   88-7800
                           CIP

For

Elizabeth, Mark, and Jenny,

who companioned and humored this effort,

as they do me;

and so made years seem like days.

TABLE OF CONTENTS

ACKNOWLEDGMENTS

Few writers, I suspect, are so delightfully ensconced as I have been, through no doing or merits of my own, for the duration of this endeavor. I owe my sojourn at Trinity College to the proverbially Irish hospitality of Professors J.M. Dillon and J.V. Luce, whose gracious initial invitation is reenacted daily in their warm collegiality. The truth is that the welcome I have received here, from among those who make up Trinity College, has too many faces to name and to appreciate now, one by one. I single out Mr. Salters Sterling and Mrs. Rosemary Doran, who alone know the extent of their assistance to my work. To all of these, I express my lasting gratitude. Finally, I thank my brother, Jim, who, in outfitting me with a computer, left me with an addiction.

Lastly, at this modest table of thanks, I set an empty place for the unnamed teachers and friends of this volume, whose number is happily beyond counting.

Robert Emmet Meagher

School of Classics
Trinity College Dublin

BIBLIOGRAPHICAL PREFACE

All of the Euripidean passages cited in this volume have one of the following three textual sources: the *Euripidis Fabulae* in the Oxford Classical Texts for all citations from Euripides' extant plays; the *Tragicorum Graecorum Fragmenta* edited by A. Nauck for all citations from Euripidean fragments, except for the one citation from the *Melanippe*, which is from volume one of *Greek Literary Papyri*, edited by D.L.Page in the Loeb series.

All translations in this volume are my own. In this regard, I wish to acknowledge and thank the University of Massachusetts Press for allowing me to draw from my translation of the *Helen*, which they have published. All centuries and specific dates cited in this volume are presumed to be B.C.E. unless otherwise noted. It should further be noted that, within this volume, in all transliterations of Greek words, the long-vowel marker [-] has been placed under and not, as is customary, over the appropriate vowels.

In my endeavor to contextualize the plays of Euripides, needless to say I have drawn upon a wide range of primary sources, which at the same time represent an ancient bibliography for the further study of Euripides. If I were to draw this focus even more tightly and select a handful of ancient sources particularly critical to the understanding of Euripides, there would be no surprises on my list: Homer (the well from which all the poets drank), Aeschylus, Sophocles, and Aristophanes (Euripides' closest colleagues), and Thucydides (the most lucid chronicler of his times). Under the rubric of secondary sources, the absence of footnotes in this volume does not mean that I am without debt. Nothing could be further from the truth, which is that my scholarly debts are too extensive to tally, much less to settle here. Scholarly footnotes, like heavy armor, are suited to doing battle but need not be strapped in place every time thinkers share their thoughts. The trappings worn by scholars all too often outweigh the scholars themselves, just as, in their writings, gloss all too often overshadows text. It is my hope that the reader will find in the absence of footnotes a less impeded path to the original texts and to the power they contain.

TABLE OF DATES

[*The titles of the extant plays of Euripides are printed here in capital letters. Symbols: ca. = around; < = before; > = after.*]

ca.534	Tragic contests established in Athens.
ca.498	Aeschylus first competes in the tragic contests.
490	Battle of Marathon.
ca.484	Birth of Euripides.
480	Battle of Salamis.
468	Sophocles first competes in the tragic contests.
456	Death of Aeschylus.
455	Euripides first competes in the tragic contests.
?<440	[RHESUS - authorship debated].
438	ALCESTIS wins second prize.
431	Beginning of Peloponnesian War; MEDEA.
430	Murder of Peloponnesian delegates without trial, perhaps reflected in the *Children of Heracles;* outbreak of plague in Athens.
?ca.429	CHILDREN OF HERACLES.
428	HIPPOLYTUS wins first prize.
427	Executions of citizens and razing of Plataea.
425	Further unspeakable savagery at Corcyra.
?ca.425	ANDROMACHE.
<423	HECUBA; with CYCLOPS ?

INTRODUCTION

Hannah Arendt prefaced her book on *Men in Dark Times* [NY:Harcourt, Brace & World, 1955] with the conviction that "even in the darkest of times we have the right to expect some illumination, and... such illumination may well come from the uncertain, flickering, and often weak light that some men and women, in their lives and works, will kindle under almost all circumstances and shed over the time span that was given them on earth... [and that] eyes so used to darkness as ours will hardly be able to tell whether their light was the light of a candle or that of a blazing sun." The very same conviction underlies this book; for Euripides wrote in times as dark as our own and shed light not only for his but for all time. Some would say that his was the light of a candle, while others would liken it to a blazing sun. Either way, and more to the point, once kindled it has never gone out.

Euripides, as a poet-playwright of the past, is known, however, only through the voice preserved in his works; and the light he kindles burns within us as we listen to his words. Now, if I were to reveal at once the crystalline core of this book by stating it as one simple claim, it would be that the prophetic clarity and intensity of Euripides' voice resound in his plays essentially undiminished by time. And if this claim, once stated, were in itself either evident or persuasive, my work would be abruptly concluded. The complication giving warrant to this book lies in the necessary reciprocity of any revelation or the fact that without ears to hear, neither falling trees nor timeless works of art can successfully resound. And hearing an ancient voice presents a unique challenge to most modern ears.

It is not as if Euripides requires the condescension of contemporary adaptation. His lords need not wear ministerial pin-

1

striped suits nor do his warriors need goose-step their way across the stage to make their meanings for us. Still less does Euripidean drama require companion lectures or program notes telling the audience what the play they are about to see or have just seen would say to them if it were still able. Such remedial interpretation is best described in Susan Sontag's words as "the compliment mediocrity pays to genius." With a theatrically vital translation and a production equal to the text, Euripides sings his own song and silences those who would presume to speak on his behalf. Such occasions, however, are rare; their rarity being no reflection on Euripides.

This book, however, addresses itself primarily to those who would **read** Euripides' plays, rather than to those who would stage or witness stage productions of them. Apart from the numerical superiority of readers, there is the fact that credible theatrical productions of ancient drama are the fruit not of improvisation but of understanding. If the director and his or her cast know and feel why they are saying what they are saying and doing what they are doing, then the audience will know and feel with them. Such is the magic of theatre. In the theatre, understanding is contagious; but so is confusion. Directors and actors, like anyone else, begin by reading a text; and reading implies a certain remove from the immediacy of theatre. Reading is an inward act, more akin to thinking than to sensing; and thinking about Euripidean drama is, before it is anything else, thinking. Theatre, on the other hand, even a theatre of ideas, outreaches thought with an ease which often angers intellectuals. No wonder that criticism has been called the intellect's revenge on art. Beyond revenge, however, there is a place for thinking about art, particularly when the art is ancient drama, which most often finds its enactment only in the solitary imagination of a reader. The reader must eventually design, direct, and act out in a theatre of thought the otherwise inert text grasped in the hands or lying open on the desk; and such collaboration with the author in the reincarnation of a once and future drama requires intense reflection. This book may be seen as one sustained series of reflections preliminary to the reading of Euripides, preliminary, that is, to the imaginative raising of the written text into dramatic life in the theatre of the imagination, wherein Euripides will speak for himself.

Although the inwardly theatrical reading of Euripides must be regarded as secondary to the actually   staged production of

Euripides, reading Euripides in private is no necessarily suspect endeavor. In fact, there are solid grounds for saying that Euripides consciously wrote for his readers as well as for his theatre audiences. The first such reader to be named is the god of the theatre, Dionysus himself, who, in the opening scene of Aristophanes' comedy, the *Frogs*, says he has been reading Euripides' *Andromeda* while on board a ship. [We may note here that, according to common practice, Dionysus, although reading alone, would have been reading aloud, a practice to be commended to any reader of Euripides.] To continue, later in the same comedy, the chorus warns that Euripides' audience come armed with their own papyrus copies of his scripts. However broad the comic license taken by Aristophanes in these instances, it is clear that even in the late fifth century Euripides had his readers and that something about Euripidean drama was perceived as inviting private reflection as well as public performance. What that something was will be explored later in some detail; but for now it may suffice to say that Euripides reflected in his work the birth of popular literacy in Athens as well as an accompanying wave of speculative and critical thinking quite foreign and threatening to long-enthroned traditions, religious, artistic, and political. There can be little doubt that much of what he had to say was quite unwelcome, if not unintelligible, to a large part of his audience. It could be argued that he could not afford to be fully understood and so masked his meanings in an irony which allowed his plays to be read either from right to left or from left to right, politically speaking, thereby shielding his words from his foes while entrusting them to his friends, wherever and whenever either might be found. As a revolutionary, fixated on the present yet essentially belonging to the future, Euripides counted on the substantiality of the written text to hold his meaning and to await its time of full disclosure.

In saying that this book is addressed primarily to those who would read Euripides' plays, I have thus far underscored the notion of reading as distinct from stage production; but equal emphasis is due the notion of the original texts, as opposed to the mountains of gloss encircling even the most slighted of his plays. There is no denying the vantages gained by scaling the heights of Euripidean scholarship or any of the surrounding peaks. However, the simple fact remains that Euripides is to be found first and finally in his own words. If Euripides was concerned to say anything at all to faces and souls he

3

knew he himself would never encounter, he must have left it somewhere in his work. After all, it is in each instance the text alone that endures and not its performance, still less its author - a fact we would scarcely assume lost on Euripides. Consequently, any reading of Euripides which is to be hopeful of understanding must trust that Euripides' meanings are present and accessible to its queries.

This trust in the possibility of more or less direct communication between the reader and Euripides mediated solely by the text, or to be both more precise and more offensive to modern methodological sensibilities, the possibility of authentic communion of the reader and Euripides in the text, underlies this book. Such trust must, however, be sobered at once by the admission that this communion is to be the fruit of labor, not of grace, much less of negligence. To say that Euripides' meanings are present and accessible is not to say that they are obvious; and to say that communication is possible is not to say with any certainty that it has actually occurred in any particular instance. Finally, it seems reasonable at such a remove to expect that bold strokes will stand out over subtleties, and that contours will be read with greater confidence than fineries. In any event, it would be unfortunate to miss or mistake the former for the latter.

The obstacles to reading the mind of Euripides are many. Like any playwright, he speaks through his characters, which is to say that he speaks with many and diverse voices, the question always remaining: which voice, if any, is his? The moral and political span of his characters could not conceivably describe the sympathies or commitments of any one man; rather, they represent a spectrum stretching, as it were, from heaven to hell. As Aristotle reports, Sophocles pointed to this same dilemma when he commented that Euripides wrote of people as they were, while he, Sophocles, wrote of people as they ought to be. Tutored by this comment, we might approach Sophocles' characters, at least his central heroic figures, with some assurance that they embody Sophocles' conceptions of excellence. With the same comment in mind, we might well despair of hearing the voice of Euripides above the cacophony of his characters. It is no wonder that Euripides' readers and audiences across the centuries have held him in such divergent repute, as political or apolitical, as radical or reactionary, as a rationalist or an

4

irrationalist, as a feminist or a misogynist, a philosopher or a phony. What we know of how Euripides' plays were originally received or subsequently regarded provides no more than opinions as unprivileged as our own regarding how Euripides himself regarded his plays and the lives and words unfolded within them. Finally, we are left with the plays themselves and our confidence that Euripides wrote them with communication in mind. "It is only shallow people," wrote Oscar Wilde, "who do not judge by appearances. The mystery of the world is the visible not the invisible." The same might be said of the lesser mystery of Euripides. Look to the text, and he will appear eventually.

A useful parallel might be drawn between the elusiveness of Euripides and the elusiveness of his younger friend, Socrates. In the *Dialogues* of Plato, we encounter a Socrates who mostly engages in what may be described as experiments. He follows the lines of others' thinking to see and to point out where they lead, without unilaterally offering his own convictions. This is not to say, however, that Socrates remains silent or neutral to the end. His experiments are at the same time contests in which there are winners and losers. In one or other Socratic manner, interlocutors who have pursued false opinions are refuted; and we are surely not misguided in searching such refutations for at least traces of Socrates' and perhaps even Plato's own thoughts on the matter. Similarly, Euripides allows his characters their own ways, as perverse as they might be; but they do not evade judgement. Consider Polymestor in the *Hecuba*. If we were to imagine for a moment that Euripides were commending the character of Polymestor even as he created him, we would measure the playwright to be a very low sort and surely no friend of women. Polymestor is, however, refuted with a vengeance. After being laid bare by Hecuba's lashing words, he is made to stand before Agamemnon and receive his unequivocal due. Borrowing an image from the prophet Isaiah, if ever there were a cup crafted for destruction by its own potter, it is Polymestor. Admittedly, not everywhere is Euripides' voice so recognizable, his own verdict so vocal. And even when it is, it is often ignored. Even Polymestor's villainy has been and will again be used against his poet-maker in a curious application of collective guilt, as if ink runs as thick as blood. More problematically, Euripides is at times enigmatically silent, even in the face of atrocities. In such moments, the search for his true

5

mind is not to be called off, however; for silence can be as eloquent as any words.

The dilemma I have just described raises a challenge that no one who would read Greek tragedy can evade, least of all a reader of Euripides. As will soon be seen in some detail, morality was the incessant preoccupation of the ancient tragedians of Athens; and morality requires not only the encountering of good and evil but the delineation and judgement of them. We cannot pretend to know what a play says or means unless we know how we are intended by the author to regard the words and actions it presents to our eyes and ears. To say this is not to eschew all complexity and ambiguity, demanding melodrama or nothing. It is simply to recognize the moral seriousness of the work we confront and the task we undertake in reading Greek tragedy. We are surely not required to match Goethe's singular reverence for Euripides when he asked, "have all the nations of the world since his day produced a single dramatist worthy of handing him his sandals?" Nonetheless, such esteem from high places might well sober efforts from lower places to dismiss or to tame his wild genius.

This book will focus on the ethical vision and voice of Euripides, because it is my conviction that there lies the core of his concerns, the point of fission. As stated above, this book will comprise a series of reflections preliminary to a dramatic reading of Euripides in the theatre of one's own imagination. These reflections will not constitute sustained critical commentaries on any, much less all, of his plays. In a book as modest as this one addressing a corpus as conspicuously manifold as the Euripidean one, there is little place for a rehearsing of the plot-lines of one drama after another, without which focused critical commentary would be deprived of context. If, on the other hand, I were to assume the reader's familiarity with the full Euripidean corpus, I would direct this book exclusively towards the classical scholar, which is far from my intent. Instead, what I propose to do is to provide what might be called a conceptual setting for the inwardly theatrical reading of Euripides.

The limitations on stage settings in the ancient theatre of Dionysus were, by our standards, severe. Generally speaking, there were only two possibilities, the palace set and the country set, each with a single central door, two side entrances, and a roof; and a playwright was not allowed to change from one set to another in the

6

course of a drama. Every Euripidean drama was thus played out against one of these two sets. Quite apart from and prior to the physical set, however, there lay what may be called a conceptual set, an ordered arrangement of categories, metaphysical and political, which, like chromosomal threads, carry and dictate the essential thought-structure of the grander, more evident organism eventually born in the open air of the orchestra. What I do not have in mind here are story-patterns or generic plot formulas which have been critically examined in considerable detail and with genuine insight in the vast literature on Euripides. The patterns or structures I would disclose lie on a deeper, more expansive level. But before we make our descent to this infra-structure of his work, we turn to Euripides himself; for it is best that he not be a stranger to us as we consider his work.

I. EURIPIDES

Ancient biographies, like any others, can be no more reliable than their sources and may, of course, be a good deal less reliable. Regretably, neither the ancient biographies of Euripides nor their sources inspire confidence. If Thucydides, committed as he was to some reasonable interrogation of hearsay and to some genuine accountability for factual accuracy, had chosen to mention Euripides, we might perhaps be in a position now to sketch more than the contours of the playwright's life. Instead, we are left mostly with legend, the presentation and assessment of which would cast very little light on our subject. A stalemate, however, in the sphere of Euripides' life, need not frustrate our endeavor to enter and understand his work; for the boldest lines of Euripides' identity are known to us and they are all we need.

We have no good reason to doubt the Parian Marble, carved roughly a century and a half after Euripides' death and citing the year 484 as the year of his birth. This is surely more plausible than the legend which would have the three great tragedians fatefully intersect each others' lives at the Battle of Salamis in the year 480: Aeschylus by fighting with the Athenian forces, Sophocles by dancing in the boys' victory chorus, and Euripides by emerging from his mother's womb. Such luminous synchronicity makes perfect poetic history. But poetic history is no more acceptable as history than is poetic justice acceptable as justice. However, a meticulous sorting out of legends and sources is too lengthy a project for our present purposes, so we must satisfy ourselves for now with reasonable assurances and approximations. With this is mind, we may say that Euripides was born in Attica in 484 and died in Macedon in 406, after emigrating to the court of Archelaus, where he likely shared the eminent company of Zeuxis the painter, Agathon the tragedian, Timotheus the musician, and possibly even Thucydides

9

the historian. Any account of his motives for quitting Athens for Macedon must be conjectured from his plays, from which one could with some confidence conjure the image of a man in despair, holding up to the people of Athens, only thinly masked, their own imminent ruin and inward rot. How far from the mind of Euripides and that of his audience could Athens have been when, in 408, in the *Orestes,* he presented the house of Agamemnon sick beyond cure and aflame with malice?

Between the years 484 and 406, apart from his endeavors as a playwright, very little is known of Euripides' activities. We may assume that he received a traditional Athenian education, that he participated to some extent in civic life and in the myriad religious festivals strung like beads on the year's cycle, and that he served his compulsory forty years of availability for active duty in the army. What is most important to realize is that Athenian playwrights neither enjoyed nor claimed exemption from the active demands of Athenian citizenship, which we would likely measure quite excessive. Even if the traditions depicting Euripides as an unsociable recluse, ensconced in a cave overlooking the Bay of Salamis, alone with his library and his pen, were in large part accurate, the truth would remain that he must have known the savagery of war, the elemental madness of the mob, the intoxication of empire, and the abysmal despair of defeat far more personally and immediately than most modern poets know the political realities impinging on or informing their work.

Those traditions which would have us believe that Euripides was scorned by the populace and hounded by his critics into exile must be set alongside the more solid facts that we have no certain evidence of his having ever been refused a chorus, that apart from Aeschlylus and Sophocles we know of no fifth-century poet so recognized and rewarded with praise, that his indictment for impiety must have been either defeated or withdrawn in a period when other equally eminent figures were not similarly spared. In addition we might consider the story told by Plutarch of how the mere recitation of lines from Euripides bought the freedom of captive Athenian warriors, otherwise rotting to death in a Sicilian quarry, or the tribute reportedly paid to Euripides by the aged Sophocles, bringing on his chorus robed in black to mourn the death of his younger colleague, or the legend claiming that the Athenian people begged the

Macedonians for the return of Euripides' bones. Finally, whatever Euripides' status in the Athenian theatre and polity during the fifth century, he was soon without rival, enjoying a preeminence reflected in the number of his plays preserved in whole or in fragments, compared to those of his once more favored rivals.

Euripides' career as a playwright began in the year 455 with the production of the trilogy including the *Peliades* and ended with the posthumous production of his *Alkmaion in Corinth, Iphigeneia in Aulis*, and *Bacchae*, after 406. The last Athenian production of his work over which he himself presided was in 408, when he presented the *Orestes*. Altogether he seems to have had twenty-two productions in the City Dionysia, the yearly theatrical festival held each spring in Athens, which would account for the sixty-six tragedies known with certainty to be from Euripides' pen and surviving either in whole or in part to this day. If we exclude the *Alcestis* from the formal category of tragedy, the more or less fully extant tragedies of indisputedly Euripidean authorship number sixteen, all from the second half of his career and all but one falling within the war years, the years of bitter internecine conflict between Athens and Sparta. The issues surrounding the composition and dating of the Euripidean canon are too complex and too peripheral to our present purposes to admit of exploration here. May it suffice to say that a quite credible case for the texts, fragmentary or whole, and their dates employed in this book could but won't be made here. In sum, it may be argued that Euripides was one of the three competing tragedians in the City Dionysia approximately every five years early in his career, every three years during his middle years; and every year towards the end of his career, often in direct competition with his senior rival, Sophocles, and with revivals of the late Aeschylus' established "classics."

However thick the mist of doubt over most of Euripides' personal characteristics, there are certain essential elements of his identity which we cannot afford to overlook, as self-evident as they may seem to be. Truisms often contain the sturdiest truths. I wish to group these essential elements under three epithets: Athenian, Scholar, and Playwright; for Euripides was undeniably all of these; and in saying this we are already saying a great deal of significance. Examining the nature of this significance is the task assigned to the remainder of this chapter.

11

EURIPIDES THE ATHENIAN

To be an Athenian citizen, Euripides had first of all to be Greek, born of Greek blood and reared in the Greek tongue; and this fact bears some preliminary consideration. All too often in classical studies, "the Greeks," at least those of the classical period, are studied in splendid isolation from those non-Greek peoples whom the classical Greeks themselves were wont to lump under the heading of "barbarians." In what might be seen as an alliance of academic parochialism and ancient racism, the extent of mutual influence among ancient East Mediterranean peoples is often all but ignored. Even the Egyptians, who by virtue of sheer topography were uniquely insulated from foreign military invasion and cultural intrusion, have seldom been handled by scholars as hermetically as have the Greeks. Increasingly, however, scholars have come to recognize the extensive mythological, ritual, iconographical, architectural, artistic, linguistic, literary, commercial, and military influences of Egypt, the Near East, and even India on Greece long before and during the period relevant to this book. Firstly, this recognition permits us to trespass stingily-drawn borders marking off those materials of legitimate interpretative relevance to Euripidean studies; and, secondly, this recognition challenges us to a deeper understanding of the chauvinism so endemic to ancient Greece and Athens and so apparently offensive to Euripides. Our own sorties across these borders will soon be in evidence; but for now the second matter, that of ancient Greek chauvinism, is of more immediate concern.

Euripides lived in a time of already established and ever-developing pan-Hellenic consciousness. What this means in simplest terms is that the word "Greek" was, in practice, felt to designate something essential, specific, and enduring. Although there was some recognition of a humanity common to all men, humanity in the flesh was too uneven and diverse and humanity in the mind too abstract to challenge the more concrete and exalted reality of being "Greek." Central among the roots of this

1 2

consciousness are surely the Homeric and Hesiodic poems, which synthesized and articulated Greek religion, virtue, and pride, as well as the Olympic, Delphic, and Isthmian pan-Hellenic festivals. Of all the catalysts of nationalism, however, paranoia is perhaps the most effective, at least if Hobbes is correct in saying that fear is the magisterial passion. The constant threat and the twice-repelled reality of barbarian invasion, once in 490 and again in 480, minted the meaning of Greek nationalism current in Euripides' era and reflected nowhere so brazenly and pathetically as in his last play, the *Iphigeneia in Aulis,* where the name of "Hellas" is repeated so often as to become a refrain, a spell-casting incantation bemusing the callow soul of Iphigeneia, who imagines herself the "savior of Greece" and willingly gives her body and soul to what is no more than a consciously fabricated abstraction, a cynical construct made by her own father who has no illusions that "Hellas" is anything more than a euphemism for the certifiably deranged mob which he leads to plunder. It is Euripides' last word on patriotism.

Levi-Strauss, for one, has pointed out how most peoples whom we are inclined to call "primitive" designate themselves as "the True Ones," "the Good Ones," or simply, "the Human Beings," and assign to the rest of men one or other name denying their humanity. This practice, however, is scarcely confined to so-called "primitives." More "advanced" peoples, such as the classical Greeks or ourselves, are more likely to dissemble than to disavow such arrogance. It is usually our methods rather than our morals which are more advanced. Thus the Greeks employed all the sophisticated tools of comparative and philosophical anthropology to develop and to support a theory of Hellenic supremacy, i.e. of Greeks as the master race. Whether as an element of fate or as an accident of climate, Greek solidarity and superiority was a common unarguable assumption in the fifth century and ready at hand to justify aggressive war, colonization, and slavery.

Euripides, however, was an Athenian Greek, which hones a sharper edge on what has been said thus far. Whatever its comparative insignificance in Bronze Age Greece, Athens emerged from the archaic period into the classical period, and more specifically into the fifth century as a military power rivalled only by Sparta and as a cultural center simply without rival in the Greek world. As pan-Hellenic consciousness developed, which is to say as Greek-speaking peoples came to think of themselves as Greeks and of the territories

1 3

they inhabited as Greece, then the emergence of its center, its capital city, might seem inevitable. Inevitably or not, in the years following the Persian Wars Athens laid claim to the full title and prerogatives of Greece's capital city; and however compromised by failure was its claim to that title in the fifth century, Athens has surely achieved it posthumously in the mind of posterity. For Athens and classical Greece are all but synonymous categories in the minds of most people inclined to think at all about such things. This is an equivalency, however, which we must learn to unthink if we are to understand Euripides and his times.

What we are calling Greece and speaking of as if it were a nation began as a make-shift confederacy of city-states hastily formed to confront the massive military might of Persia and its empire. After the trousered barbarian hordes had twice been repelled from Greek soil, Athens argued that the alliances so hastily and provisionally formed under pressure of invasion should be formalized and bolstered so as to provide for the lasting security of Greece against future threats from its enemies. Understating the part played by Sparta as well as by chance in their victories and overstating the admittedly critical part played by itself, Athens crowned itself the "Savior of Hellas," and proceeded to form a new confederation centered in and administered from Athens. In short, Athens presented itself as the first city among its equals; but soon enough the monster emerged and its true designs clicked into place. The confederacy became an empire, peers became subjects, and Greece became a euphemism for the sphere of Athenian hegemony. Appropriately enough, this devolution from a consortium of friends to an empire of subjects is mirrored in Menelaus' account of Agamemnon's rise to primacy in the *Iphigeneia in Aulis;* and we may be hearing an echo of Euripides' own rage at Athens in the words of Menelaus thrown at the pathetically compromised Agamemnon: "I indict you first for those ways in which you first proved yourself perverse."[349] Athens' coup, however, was soon challenged by Sparta, itself only slightly less attracted to empire. The result was civil war with Greek unity sliced every which way as both Athens and Sparta seduced and strangled individual city-states into taking sides. Like the sons of Oedipus in the *Phoenician Women*, Athens and Sparta, rivals for a single rule, each pursued one of twin evils and created a two-headed madness.

14

The "Savior of Hellas," in short, became "the tyrant city"; and like all tyrants its fall from grace was followed by its fall from power. "Mortal man plays the fool when he wastes cities, desecrates temples, and leaves desolate the holy places of the dead. His own ruin is not far off."[*Trojan Women*,95-97] The same is easily said, blown large as it were, for cities. It is not difficult to say from Euripides' plays which fall, the moral or the military, he found more painful to witness. We may be allowed to hear Euripides' own sentiments echoed in these words from the *Phoenician Women*: "It would seem that one's homeland is of all things the dearest. - Yes, there are no words to describe how dear it is."[406-407] Indeed, in Euripides' earlier extant plays, such as the *Medea*, the *Children of Heracles*, and the *Suppliant Women*, there may be evidence of how dearly Euripides once held his native Athens; for the image of Athens in those plays is of a "holy, inviolate land" [*Medea*,825-826], a land where freedom, wisdom, and harmony flourish, a land always ready to defend the weak and the wronged. These early portraits of Athens, however, soon bore little resemblance to the tyrant city; and Euripides' later portrayals of his city were as ragged and ruthless as the reality demanded.

The story of Athens' precarious rise to power and its fall therefrom is told nowhere with such poignancy as in Thucydides' history of *The Peloponnesian War*, which work could well be listed among the ancient tragedies, despite the scale of its stage, the multiplicity of its characters, and the absence of poetic diction. It presents the tragedy of Athens which offers perhaps the most shattering *peripeteia* in history, the tragic reversal of Athens' fortunes from its Periclean splendor to its Sicilian devastation, and does so by underscoring the gulf that existed between Athens' words and deeds, a gulf opening nowhere more abysmally than between the words of promise pronounced by Pericles over the casualties of the war's first year and the debacle consummated in the quarries of Sicily. This chasm between Athenian rhetoric and reality, possibility and outcome, words and deeds, was witnessed daily by Athenians, like Euripides and Thucydides, possessing sufficient insight and integrity to read their times with perception. Finally, we will see that it is precisely this contemporary tragedy of Athens, unmasked in Thucydides, that is so thinly masked in myth by Euripides in so many of his plays.

In sum, to be an Athenian in the second half of the fifth century was to live and to be complicit in a city at war, a shameless, wasteful war of aggression. It was to watch one's homeland take on all of the distortions of monstrous bad faith, to listen as words changed their meanings to suit otherwise unspeakable wrongs, to be sick not only with the plague bacillus that ravaged Athens in the first years of the war but to be sick as well with the even more unsparing human plague that was the war itself.

However deeply the war marked, or rather scarred, Athens in the Euripidean period, war does not alone tell her story. The shadow cast by war could not eclipse and may in fact have partly provoked what has been called the Athenian "Enlightenment," a period of turbulent questioning, revaluation, and discovery. This was the age of the Sophists, an uneasily defined collage of free-thinkers, who despite their reputation for itineracy mostly made their home in Athens. Their widely divergent teachings are not readily synthesized; for they were never a school or a church with any commitment to consensus or to a common doctrine. Generally, however, we may say that they promoted free, empirical inquiry and found an adaptable, humanistic viewpoint to be the most revealing one. They were no friends of the traditional poets, Homer first among them, whom they found to be at best deceived and at worst deceitful, particularly with respect to the gods and their Olympian morals, or lack thereof. Central to their concerns were education, ethics, and theology, concerns which they shared with Euripides.

The fifth-century "Enlightenment" was hardly created by or confined to the Sophists, however. Scientific and philosophical speculation which had begun long before the fifth century and which in some instances had originated outside of Greece converged in Athens and came to fruition there. Foundational, as well, to the upheaval of this time was the emergence of popular literacy, which conspired with and supported the contemporary free-thinkers in breaking forever the spell of Homer and of traditional oral education. The profound link between literacy and individual freedom is by now a datum of political experience. The acquisition of literacy, it is well known, brings not only a new skill but a new frame of mind. And in fifth-century Athens that new frame of mind meant, for one, the

16

emergence of an autonomous individuality quite foreign to archaic Greece. Antique notions of retribution, inherited guilt, pollution, and predestination were called into question; and new theories of compassion, forgiveness, altruism, intentionality, and free will were forged. New theologies as well as imported cults responded to and generated the longing and hope for personal salvation, just as confidence in the cosmos collapsed. Human reason and its moral affirmations came to be seen by many not as an always imperfect confession of the flawless divine order but as a humane, even defiant, alternative to the callous indifference of the given order of things. Nature and law formed no longer an uncontested unity. Clearly, however, there can be no full chronicling here of the intellectual and political uprisings of the fifth century. May it suffice for now to say that Euripides was in the middle of them.

Finally, there is perhaps no more telling indication of the depth of questioning in fifth century Athens than the fact that it reached even to the institution of slavery, both those slaves captured in battle or purchased in the market and the slaves which Greek law and custom made of all women. It is in the theatre of Euripides that we hear the first indication that there may be something unnatural in chattel slavery; and it is equally clear from his plays that every aspect of women's relationship to men and to male society is under radical review. In this and in numerous other respects, Euripidean drama holds an unmerciful mirror to the face of Athens in the fifth century. Like the acceptance of bold and brilliant pigment on the sublimely blanched sculptures of ancient Athens, so the acceptance of radical turbulence and controversy in the ancient theatre of Euripides may demand that we shatter and recast more familiar conceptions of ancient tragedy and of its mother-city, conceptions more compatible with Aeschylus, Sophocles, and Aristotle.

EURIPIDES THE SCHOLAR

The epithet "scholar" may seem to be an unlikely one for Euripides; and it is used here, admittedly, for lack of something better. To denote the qualities which I have in mind to discuss now under this heading, others have preferred "philosopher" or "thinker"

17

or "Sophist" or even "bookworm," all of which seem at least a shade further from the mark than "scholar," provided that we rid our minds of any formally academic associations with the word; for whatever Euripides was, he was not a schoolman or an academician.

Reference has already been made to the emergence of popular literacy in the late fifth-century. The claim has also been made that literacy brings with it a new frame of mind and freedom of thought. These elements and more, as we shall see, figure centrally in the theatre of Euripides and form the cluster of qualities towards which the name of "scholar" imperfectly gestures.

Tradition suggests that Euripides possessed a personal library of extraordinary size for his day; and his plays give ample evidence of a mind both traditionally learned and immediately engaged in the most current intellectual debates. Interestingly, he wrote not only for readers but also about readers; for written texts play a decisive role in several of his extant dramas. For example, in the surviving second rendering of the *Hippolytus*, it is in a note penned by the suicidal Phaedra that Hippolytus is falsely charged with attempted seduction; and the written word, in this instance, receives credence over Hippolytus' spoken protestations of his own innocence. Death's silence is, it seems, not final; and Theseus prefers to find the truth in what he reads than in what he hears. The written word proves equally ineradicable and deadly in the *Iphigeneia in Aulis*; for it is the first fatal letter to Clytemnestra which Agamemnon is attempting the re-draft as the play opens. But neither the original draft of the letter nor the fate of Iphigeneia which it deceivingly prescribes admits of revision. The written word unwittingly effects a brighter event in the *Iphigeneia in Tauris*, however, wherein Euripides constructs the most lengthy and elaborate recognition scene in Greek tragedy around a letter dictated by the illiterate Iphigeneia to one of her more learned and less fortunate victims. In short, literacy - the reading and writing of texts - is thematically explicit and crucial, uniquely so, in Euripidean drama.

More significant, however, than the literal presence of the act and artefacts of literacy, is the presence of what I have referred to as the frame of mind and freedom of thought accompanying literacy. Far more learned and lucid accounts than any I might offer here have already been written describing the psychology and epistemology of oral education and oral culture; but some account of this matter must

1 8

be presented here as well. Both the recitation and the reception of unwritten poetry, preserved nowhere if not in the memories of bard and audience, require an uncritical, unhesitating mimetic surrender to the sung sounds and rhythms. "Hearing" may well be unwilling and unconscious, since the ear has no lids as do the eyes to preclude intrusion; but mere hearing is unlikely to result in the precise remembering of what was heard, particularly if the sounds inadvertently overheard comprise thousands of lines of complex poetry. School children would be a good deal more learned than they generally are if memory were effective regardless of the quality of one's hearkening. Memory requires listening; and listening involves a simple giving over of oneself, as any phenomenology of listening readily reveals. It is no linguistic accident that the Greek word *akouein* means both to listen and to obey; for soundful communication, unfolding as it does across time, must be followed as if it were a command. Indeed, poetic recitation or story-telling may be said to constitute a mode of command, a command to surrender the free movement of one's own thoughts to the poet's words so that the latter might unfold freely. Any intrusion of one's own doubts and concerns foreign to the pure flow of the sung or recited poem is as destructive to the life of the poem as is an embolism in the bloodstream of a living organism. Oral communication, in short, cannot tolerate interruption, a point made by Socrates on more than one occasion and a fact illustrated more recently, in 1830, by a man named Moerenhout, who wrote of his encounter with an old Tahitian cantor, a holy man, who recited for him the Polynesian cosmogony. The cantor could only declaim the tale spontaneously in one unbroken flow. Each time Moerenhout interrupted the cantor so as to write down that portion of the myth just sung, the cantor lost his song altogether and had to begin again from the beginning in order to regain it.

Whether in nineteenth-centry (A.D.) Tahiti or fifth-century Greece, oral cultures are obliterated by the introduction of writing. Memory is no longer necessary for the preservation of learning and the spell cast by song over the listener is broken. The text, now visible and substantially independent, lies before and between teacher and learner, at their mutual disposal and no longer beyond critique. Texts, unlike recitations, are ever open to challenge, critique and discussion. In an oral tradition, what is forgotten is lost

19

forever; and the fact that, as Levi-Strauss points out, the tradition is transformed in the belief that it is only being repeated never fully comes to light. With the introduction of the written text, however, multiple variant versions of a single myth or poem may be preserved and critically compared, both with each other and against other sources. In the visual realm of the written text, the inquiring, discursive mind may range over the text at its own pace and selecting its own directions, just as the eye is free to focus wherever it wishes and to consider from a variety of perspectives the visual object, permanently at its disposal. In fact, the freedom of the eye provides numerous parallels with the freedom of reason consequent upon the collapse of orality.

It has been said that the Socratic question *ti estin* ?, the question "what is the nature of...?", dismantled Greek mythical thinking, a form of thinking which had prevailed in the archaic age and well into the classical period until the time of the Sophists. Whatever truth there may be to such a claim, it must be added that Socrates exemplified his times at least as fully as he shaped them. Semonides' new art of memory, developed in the late sixth century, seems to have been predominantly visual; and Empedocles, not many years later, stressed the acquisition of knowledge through a variety of the senses. Surely the ground beneath orality is softened by both of these contributions. Similarly, the development of critical prose and its gradual replacing of poetry as the most serious vehicle of thought began with medical and philosophical treatises, chronicles and speeches, well before Socrates, who, after all, to our knowledge never wrote a page.

Not only the Socratic dialogues but the dramas of Euripides, as well, are replete with questions and speculations regarding the nature of things. Consider, for one, the following choral selections from Euripides' *Helen* [1137-1144;1148-1150):

What is god?
What is not god?
What lies in between?
What man can say
He has reached the edges of existence,
No matter where he has been?
What man has gazed upon god,

Witnessed the wild confusion at the core of things,
The contradictions,
The unexpected twists of fate,
And returned to tell the tale?

There is nothing sure
In all the turnings of men's minds.
Only god's words are bright with truth.

If free critical inquiry, open cultural debate, and linguistic experimentation mark the collapse of oral culture and of mythical thinking, then Euripidean drama is as fertile a field as any in which to trace the movement from hearing to seeing, or from the reliving of tradition in memory to the critical examination of tradition in the often harsh light of reason. The story that Socrates attended the theatre only when he could see the works of Euripides testifies at the very least to the perceived congeniality of these two, Socrates the philosopher and Euripides the playwright. After all, in the *Frogs*, Euripides is accused of having thrown out music for the sake of hair-splitting arguments, which is not far afield from charges laid against Socrates then and ever since. Euripides played far more free with metrical codes than did his predecessors, frequently obscuring the distinction between sung and unsung lines or between what was traditionally reserved for the chorus and what was reserved for actors, and bringing the language of his dialogues into closer coincidence with ordinary colloquial discourse. He may hardly be accused with any justice, however, of abandoning music; for the music of his plays is rich and luxuriant. In his time, Euripides was associated with the "new music" exemplified by Timotheus; and in any age there are those who say of the new music that it is simply not music. Perhaps Euripides' most exotic musical innovations were the astrophic, polymetric monodies of his late plays, such as that of Ion's temple-tidying entry in the *Ion* and that of the Phrygian slave's frenzied account of mayhem in the *Orestes*.

The Socratic character, if we may call it that, of Euripides' plays, however, runs deeper than their mutual liberation from metrical conventions. The Euripides of the *Frogs* [971ff] admits without apology that he has introduced his audience to thinking, even taught them how to think [*phronein*] by presenting characters who

21

question, reason, and debate whatever happens and whatever they do. And we see for ourselves in his plays how appropriate is this admission. It is all but unheard of, for instance, in earlier non-Euripidean tragedies for central characters to change their minds, whereas Euripides presents us with a gallery of characters who painfully reconsider and reverse their actions. On occasion the entire structure of a play is woven by the interplay of two or more characters changing their minds in tragic syncopation, most notably perhaps in the *Hippolytus* and in the *Iphigeneia in Aulis*. Socrates must have been more than once edified by the extent to which Euripidean characters, or some at least, led the examined life. Furthermore, we find Euripides' characters often talking to themselves, wondering how things have turned out as they have or why they themselves are going to do what they are indeed about to do.

If we knew of Euripides only from Aristophanes, we might imagine that Euripides squeezed his plays from books, which is far from the truth. It remains true, however, that Euripidean prologues are sometimes quite bookish and that his characters are known to break out into discourses better suited to school than to stage. The most current and pressing intellectual and political debates of his day find voice in his tragedies, for example the debate over the meaning and relative status of natural law versus convention, or the debates over the demythologization of Greek religion, the secular critique of civic religion and of folk piety, the merits of democracy and the ethics of empire. Indeed, such contemporarily charged issues as the death of god, women's liberation, radical theology, the military-industrial complex, economic imperialsim, and de-colonization would be foreign to Euripides only as terms, not as ideas. For someone who has been said to have composed his poetry in a cave and to have shunned the throng of the city, Euripides could not have been more in the thick of things. Associating, as he seems to have done, with Anaxagoras, Protagoras, Prodicus, and Socrates, he was both at the center and on the edge of his times; for his was a city both productive and intolerant of change, a city disposed to disown and to dispatch, in one way or another, its most legitimate progeny. "The best traditions make the best rebels," wrote Gilbert Murray in *Euripides and His Age*. [Oxford, 1946] "Euripides is the child of a strong and splendid tradition and is, together with Plato, the fiercest of all rebels against it."

22

In sum, Euripidean theatre constituted an open forum for a deeply divided society to display its divisions, if nothing else. The famous Protagorean dictum that there are two sides to every argument and the accompanying suggestion that a clever man ought to be able to argue either side successfully give rise and shape to one battle of words after another in Euripidean drama. In these moments of rhetorical pyrotechnics Euripides is presenting, as it were, to his audience's gaze and for their consideration the pragmatic manipulation of language to suit and dissemble one's purposes, a skill central to the Sophist curriculum and prevalent in the politics of empire. It would be an unthinking response to these moments in his plays, however, to imagine that Euripides' theatrical fascination and facility with Sophistic rhetoric indicate the location of his true sympathies. Closer, I would propose, to the sympathies of Euripides are these words of Agamemnon in the *Iphigeneia in Aulis* [333]: "The clever [*sophe_*] tongue I find hateful and malignant." There are many "clever tongues" in Euripides' plays, making every effort to cover the stench of their deeds with the perfume of their words; but as a rule they do not fare well. One such smooth tongue, as we have already seen, belongs to Polymestor in the *Hecuba*; and, translated freely, Hecuba's raw response [1187ff] comes down to this: There is nothing worse than rot wrapped in finery. Behind whatever veil of words, however finely woven, a rotten life begins to smell and give itself away. The same Hecuba is no kinder to Helen in the *Trojan Women* [969ff] when Helen talks for her life, making over her deeds more thickly than, presumably, she ever had to make over her face. Without exhausting ourselves here with citations, we may say that this confrontation of words with the deeds that cower behind them is too common and central to Euripidean drama to escape anyone's notice and might be seen to present a critique of Sophistic rhetoric, or of its abuse at the very least. And, if that is the case, then we are justified in hearing the voice of Euripides himself in this fragment [N2.439]: "How I wish that facts could speak for themselves, so that they could not be misrepresented by eloquence."

Facts or actions, however, do not speak. They have no voice of their own and thus must find eventual voice in words which reveal them faithfully. Consequently, the battle for truth comes down to a contest of words, a contest between true words and false words, words which are transparent to deeds and words which are an opaque screen dissembling the deeds that lurk behind them. "The account born out of truth is simple and straightforward, standing in no need of elaborate interpretation. It makes its own case. But the word with no justice on its side is simply sick to its core and needs whatever tonics cleverness might concoct." [*Phoenician Women*,469-472] This is essentially the claim of Medea, who, after listening to Jason painting a halo around his sins, confronts him and says to him with utter confidence "one word is all it will take to stretch you out flat." [*Medea*,585]

The Aristophanic Euripides confessed proudly that he let everyone talk; and we might add that he let them say whatever they pleased. But to speak is not necessarily to have the final word. Refutation was often swift to follow, delivered, as we have seen, directly by another's words, more revealing of the truth. The forms of refutation in Euripidean drama are many. In the *Hecuba*, Polymestor is first contradicted, even as he speaks, by a mere stage prop, the shrouded remains of the boy whom he cut down and cast into the sea but whom he says is even now as safe as safe can be. Thinking that the corpse before him is that of Hecuba's last surviving girl, Polymestor is smug and sure that his words are working their wanted effect; but, to the ears of Hecuba and of the audience, Polymestor's words make no more sound than pennies dropped into a bottomless well. His fate is sealed. Rather more subtle is the refutation meted out to Orestes whose own words are made to mock him [*Orestes*,646-651]:

> All right, I committed a crime. Even so, it
> would be criminal of you not to commit a crime
> now to help me out. After all, it was criminal
> of my father Agamemnon to muster an army and
> throw it against Troy. But he wasn't exactly
> doing anything wrong, because the wrong he was
> doing was done to make right the wrong that
> your wife did, which was criminal. Anyway, you
> owe me a wrong, Menelaus, for the wrong done
> rightly for you.

This gibberish poured from the mouth of Orestes is surely no critique of moral discourse; rather it is a parody of the sophisticated but futile disfiguration of language to conceal rather than to reveal the truth. In retrospect now, it may be more accurate to speak of Euripidean theatre's presenting not so much an open forum for the mere airing of diverse opinions as a courtroom wherein the decisive debates of his age might be adjudicated. In the Euripidean theatre, it is closer to the truth to say that Athens is on trial than to say that Athens is on display. The most obscure aspect of this trial, of course, is the identity of the judge. Here Euripides fades behind his characters, just as Plato fades behind Socrates, who, in turn, is as elusive a figure as we are likely to meet anywhere. Perhaps all we are able to say in the absence of directly imparted Socratic or Euripidean doctrine is that some opinions are better than others and that our eyes are rather more discerning after our reading of Euripides or Socrates than before. In sum, the claim I am making comes down to this: the playwright, as Euripides lives the calling, is no less committed than is the philosopher to truth: to the telling of the truth if possible, to the untelling of lies if necessary, and to the admission of ignorance if ignorance is all that seems available. Perhaps this is where scholarship rightly ends: with the exhaustion, in both senses, of ignorance.

EURIPIDES THE PLAYWRIGHT

Our discussion of Euripides as playwright is admittedly already underway and will reach to the last page written here. Consequently, the agenda of this rather slight subsection requires a modest focus, which is simply this: to come to some provisional understanding of the place of the playwright in fifth-century Athens. In what terms, we might ask, was the calling of the playwright understood? What were the expectations placed on him? By what standards was he measured?

To put first things first, we may turn to Plato, whom anyone would agree was a man with priorities. Interestingly, Plato, in the *Republic*, which along with Aristophanes' *Frogs* comprises the richest ancient source for our present discussion, makes no distinction between poets and playwrights or, more specifically, between Homeric poetry and Attic drama. In this light, Euripides stands in a direct line with Homer, and tragedy constitutes an Attic supplement to Homer. In this as in other matters, we may assume that Plato was overlooking the realm of appearances and striking what he saw to be the essential underlying unity of epic and tragic poetry.

The essence shared by epic and tragic poetry is education, which we must take to mean public or political education in the sense of the education of the polis. No one would quarrel with the altogether central place of Homeric poetry in the traditional education of the Greeks, who learned not only to speak but also to think and to act as Greeks through the mimetic absorption of Homeric verse. Homeric poetry has been described as the "tribal encyclopaedia" of ancient Hellas; and it is as such that Plato confronts and challenges it. Tragic drama, on the other hand, far from encyclopaedic in scope, comprises mere "slices" from the Homeric whole, served as what might be regarded as "tea" in comparison with the Homeric feast. For Plato, however, only the scale is different. Tragic poetry, no less than epic poetry, possesses as its defining function education.

It was not until Plato's founding of the academy, consequent upon his moral despair of not only Athens but any city likely ever to emerge in stone and flesh, that education ceased, in principle as it were, to be the business of the city and became the business of a precinct apart, an intellectual *temenos* known as the academy. In the fourth century, the charge of education passed, at least in theory, from civic culture to formal schooling, which Plato understood to be inevitably counter-cultural. Civic education, the education depicted in the parable of the cave, is, in Plato's estimation, invariably miseducation. For our purposes, however, what is essential to notice is that Plato's attempted and largely successful coup in the *Republic* takes as its incontestable point of departure the double fact that the city is the first to instruct its citizens and that the poets are the first to instruct the city. Otherwise, the massive intellectual effort of Plato to wrench education away from the city and his directing of that effort straight at the poets would have to be seen as unmitigated strategic folly.

Plato's conception of dramatic poetry as essentially instructional is not to be seen as a Platonic idiosyncrasy. After all, tragic poetry was supported by elaborate civic patronage in Athens. No less than the construction and fitting-out of a warship for the

Athenian fleet, the subsidizing of a tragic production constituted a *leitourgia,* the discharging of a serious and economically onerous service to the city. We might also point to the fact that the specific word for playwright or dramatic poet in classical Greek is *didascalos,* "teacher" or "instructor". Admittedly, this term points primarily to the playwright's task of teaching his play to the chorus and the actors assigned to him by the civic authorities. Nevertheless, it may be argued that the sphere of the playwright's teaching extended beyond the cast to the city; and such an argument would find solid support in the *Frogs,* to which we turn next.

Aristophanes, like Plato, must be cited with circumspection regarding Euripidean drama; but, in the case of both, we are on rather more solid ground when our focus falls not on the points they are arguing but rather on what they assume as common knowledge or opinion in arguing their peculiar points. In the *Frogs,* both Aeschylus and Euripides, who agree on precious little, have no cause to quarrel with the claim that tragic poets like themselves are "teachers of men." More precisely, what is affirmed in the *Frogs* is that poets, in their capacity as teachers, give counsel not to children but to youths, those who are on the brink of manhood. Poets preside, as it were, over an essential rite of passage from childhood to manhood. Elsewhere, the same would-be men receive from the city their military training and their first assignments as "ephebi," what we might call "recruits." The "basic training" provided by the theatre is directed not at muscle and nerve but at the mind and the heart. The young Athenian male, at eighteen, was to be made ready not only for the challenges of war but also for the challenges of citizenship. Not only did his chaotically passionate flesh and spirit require the tempering of rigorous discipline; but his callow, impressionable, intemperate soul, like hot wax, required the stamp of the city. In Athens, it was the poet's charge to cut that seal and to impress it upon each new generation of citizens. In short, before the inauguration of "higher education" by Plato, the poets and, in the fifth century, preeminently the tragic poets were the "teachers of men" in the sense of teachers who make men of boys.

The "rite of passage" over which the poet presides is that between the private realm and the public realm. The primary identification of the Athenian boy was with his family, tribe, and constiitutional district or "deme"; but with manhood one became in the fullest sense an Athenian, whose essential loyalties and commitments were expected to transcend personal and familial considerations. At approximately the age of six, a boy was weaned a second time from his mother and removed from the women's quarters to the men's quarters where he would take his meals and associate primarily with his own sex. At the age of eighteen, however, a young man was removed from his home altogether and sent off for military training and his first tour of duty. This is the critical age, the critical point of turning, wherein a young man first enters the service of his city and discovers what may be called the public or common realm as distinct from the private realm. Thucydides likened the ancient city or polity to a common meal, a "pot-luck" we might call it, to which each citizen brings not only his hunger but also his contribution. It is to this feast that the poet invites the youth, counselling him regarding not only what he might reasonably expect of the city but also what the city might reasonably expect of him.

In the theatre of Dionysus, the stakes, as it were, could not have been higher for the city of Athens. Admittedly, the tragic curriculum was not so expansive as to challenge the Homeric encyclopaedia on every front. Instead, the tragic curriculum struck at the heart and the mind and the eyes, leaving the extremities to be instructed elsewhere. The core of the tragic curriculum was political and moral, not as distinct categories but as essentially complementary dimensions of a single wisdom or skill, which Plato's Protagoras calls "political wisdom [*sophia politice*] or "political skill" [*politice techne*]. The three constitutive elements of this wisdom or skill, as explicated in the *Protagoras*, are: firstly, the skill of waging war [*techne polemice*]; secondly, a sense of justice or right action [*dike*]; and , thirdly, a sense of honor or shame [*aidos*]. The art of warfare, the effective employment of violence, was required in mythic or prehistoric times to secure the human realm from bestial threats, in fact to turn the tables and make man the predator instead of the prey. The art of waging war, however, which is not the subject matter of tragedy, is itself a threat to the polity which possesses it; for it may at any time turn inward. Like fire, it is civilizing; but also like fire it must be contained or it will cook more than meat and will consume the very dwelling whose construction was made possible by the tools shaped and tempered in its flames. In short, any city may wage war against other cities or even with itself; and we know from Athenian history

28

and literature that civil war was indeed the Athenian political nightmare *par excellence*. What contains within acceptable limits the destructive potential of systematic human violence are the two other essential elements of civic wisdom or skill: a sense of justice and a sense of shame; and these are instilled, etched into the souls of Athenian youth, by the poets whose words must be hot and bright with truth.

It is further claimed in the *Protagoras* that cities cannot be formed unless political wisdom is the possession of all or nearly all citizens. Political wisdom cannot be the prerogative or the burden of a minority, if cities and thus specifically human life are to survive and flourish. Protagoras goes so far as to place in the mouth of Zeus himself the following decree, thus giving it the highest of sanctions: "If anyone proves incapable of participating in a [common] sense of justice and shame, let him be put to death as one who is a plague to his city." [*Protagoras,*322d] Shameless immorality is not only destructive but contagious, and cannot be tolerated. With this in mind, we approach an understanding of how profoundly serious was the calling of the poet, the teacher of citizens, above all the youngest citizens. To betray that calling was to corrupt the young and to threaten the city no less than if one had laid seige to its walls.

This calling, to teach the city of Athens, is not in question when Aeschylus and Euripides square off in the *Frogs*. What is in question is the curriculum. Their quarrel is not over their responsibility to teach, but rather over what it is they ought to teach and how they ought to teach it. Since our concern here is with Euripides, we will focus on his proposals. He says that his teachings ought to be eminently practical and decent, serving to enhance life in the city, all of which may be conveyed by the word *chresta* [1057]. Furthermore, Euripides suggests that the manner of his speech should suit its message. A simple, straightforward, humanizing lesson is best conveyed in simple, straightforward terms. What he has to say must, in his word, be said *anthropeios* [1057], by which he must mean something like: "in simplest human terms." It would seem, then, at least as an experiment, premised on the possibility that Aristophanes is conveying with some faithfulness the acknowledged purpose of the poet in Athens, that we might approach the work of Euripides as that of a man endeavoring to counsel his fellow citizens regarding justice and honor and shame, the most fundamental human decencies, without which common life may not survive much less flourish, and doing so in those terms most likely, in his judgement, to convey without distortion his central teaching. If we add to this his realization that he was endeavoring to counsel a city already corrupt, already plagued with cival war and fraternal slaughter, already festering with private violence, then we might approach the work of Euripides as that of a teacher with an unwelcome teaching, forced to deploy strategies of ironic indirection to insure that his teaching will come out straight. We might even conjecture that Euripides, aware that his words were often acid poured on open wounds and cognizant of the time that the written word could now buy for premature proposals, wrote for the future, for any time and place in which he might be understood.

After all, we may recall the perhaps presumptuous claim of Pericles, reported for us in Thucydides' history of *The Peloponnesian War*, to the effect that Athens was the school for all of Hellas, the standard measure for all the cities of Greece. And, as if this were too modest an achievement, Pericles predicted that future ages would wonder at Athens even as did his own age. Regretably, Pericles the visionary proved strangely blind to the shamefulness and injustice of greed and self-agrandizement on the part of a city, though he was the first to condemn them on the part of any citizen. Cities, he seemed to imagine, lay beyond the bounds of ethics. In fact, he seems to have argued quite openly that cities like Athens with imperial designs and responsibilities cannot afford to display decency, pity, or compassion. Somehow he dreamed that domestic policy and foreign policy could be sealed off hermetically from each other and that the splendor of the one could ignore and outshine the filth of the other. In this he proved himself a fool, with the result that future ages wonder at Athens not only for its culture but for its corruption, as well.

In sum, Athens was the teacher of Greece and, in some measure, of all ages; and Euripides was in the front ranks of the teachers of Athens. Singularly sighted in those darkened areas wherein Pericles and his city appear to have been all but blind, Euripides teaches us about all that shone and about all that stank in a city, which for the sheer scale of its accomplishments, good and evil, has few rivals. In the works of Euripides, we wonder indeed at Athens, its civilization and its barbarity, and perhaps even more at their coexistence; and, unless we place the dramas of Euripides under glass and gaze at them squintingly, as we would at a series of laboratory slides, we will wonder too at how little has changed. In the theatre of Euripides, the tragedy behind the tragedies is always that of Athens, in its particularity and its universality, the timeless tragedy of the path not taken, of lost potential, of what might have been. It is the tragedy we hear in the voice of Adrastus in the *Suppliant Women* [949-954], sick to death with the pointless suffering we humans cause each other:

> O wretched race of mortals,
> Why slaughter each other with your spears?
> Stop all this and lighten the load you bear.
> Settle down with each other into lives of kindness,
> And let your cities be secure in this.
> For life is a brief business.
> Better to make it as easy as you can,
> Then to go through it
> Bent over with pain.

In the *Laws*, Plato looks back at the decline of Athens and says that it was when the populace, rather than the best and wisest among them, were allowed to judge the theatrical and musical contests that the city fell apart. Presumably, what he means is that the populace wished above all to be entertained, flattered in their fantasies, confirmed in their prejudices. Regardless, what is surprising in Plato's comment is not that he attributes the decline of theatre to the arguably vulgar judgement of the people-at-large, but that he attributes the decline of the city to the decline of its theatre. It is interesting in this context that Dionysus in the *Frogs* says that he is in search of a poet because the city needs saving, as if a poet might do more than a god for a city on the skids. There was an ancient saying among the Greeks that "a city deserted by its gods is a city lost." [Aeschylus, *Seven Against Thebes*, 217-218] There may be some truth, then and now, to saying the same of a city and its poets. The theatre, after all, as we shall consider in the next chapter, was the city's "seeing place," the place of vision; and when the theatre falls upon dark times, the city goes blind.

II. THEATRE

The foregoing discussion of the playwright's place and profession in Athenian public life already frames the forthcoming discussion of the place and function of theatre. The theatre was, quite simply, the locus and the medium of the tragic poet's teaching. As its name suggests, it was a "seeing-place," which is not to deny the aural, musical dimension of drama but only to give preeminence to the dimension of sight. This primacy of sight requires critical and speculative consideration, because in it lies the key to the interpretation of tragedy set forth in this volume. Consequently, we turn first to a consideration of the sight proper and peculiar to theatre.

In our earlier contrasting of seeing and hearing, we noticed the freedom of the eye in ranging over the visual object, which remains at the more or less stable disposal of the see-er. In addition to the relative independence of the eye, we may notice too the essential commonality of sight. Whether we consult formal studies of sight, ancient and modern, or whether we consult directly our own everyday experience of sight, we come eventually to the common-sense conclusion that ordinary objects of sight and our ordinary sight of them are reliably common to all sighted individuals. Despite the uneven quality of individual vision, the exceptional instances of optical illusion, and the inescapable particularity of perspective, we experience sight as the most common of the senses. Even those who have been intellectually or spiritually persuaded in theory that the visual world is illusory or radically private rely in practice from day to day on seeing their way through a shared world. Quite simply, if I were to see an object in open sight and point it out to others around me, only to find that I alone see it, I would be confounded rather than confirmed in my convictions; and I propose that I am far from being alone in this.

To say that the Athenian theatre was a seeing-place, then, assigns it to the common realm. The circular construction of the

33

Greek theatre and the placing of the drama in the middle of that circle at the more or less equal disposal of all citizens further suggests that theatre belonged to the public realm. It was not a place where privilege or power determined the degree of one's participation. Rather, being a place of common sight, it was necessarily a place of freedom and equality. As such, it was an integral component and expression of Athenian public life. Like the pnyx where all citizens were permitted an equal voice and an equal vote, and like the agora, where all citizens had equal access by lot to service in the highest deliberative and judicial bodies, and like the acropolis, where public sacrifices for the well-being of all citizens were performed not by an ensconced priesthood but again by citizens, like all of these foci of Athenian life the theatre was defined as a public realm designed and designated for an essentially common experience, in this case the experience of a common vision. The orchestra, then, no less than the common civic hearth in the agora and the common civic altar on the acropolis, was a central symbol of the polis and a vital source of its life. In fact, I would claim that Attic tragedy, an art form nearly native to Athens, was a foundationally constitutive element of the democratic Athenian polis.

It is clearly beyond the bounds of this discussion to trace a path from Mycenaean monarchy to Athenian democracy. Nonetheless, we should be aware that the acropolis of Athens no longer vaunted a royal palace in the fifth century; rather, the place of the ancient kings belonged now to the gods. And in the common worship of their gods, Athenian citizens acknowledged not only their inequality with the gods but also their equality with each other. Ritual sacrifice, as we shall see in some detail later, was the cornerstone of Greek religion, and served to delineate the divine from the human, the sacred from the profane. The absolute, authoritative word of the divine or divinely representative ruler, which formed the basis of nearly all ancient East Mediterranean regimes, found no place in Athens, nor, in principle did the rule of force. Both the sceptre and the spear, authority and force, the two rival principles of rule represented by Agamemnon and Achilles, respectively, in their bitter quarrel depicted by Homer, both were rejected by Athenian democracy. In the *Iliad*, Zeus alone possessed both absolute authority and absolute power; and it may be argued that even Homer, who is said to have given to the Greeks both their gods and their heroes, finally rejected both the sceptre and the spear as the bases of human fellowship, when he had Achilles and Priam reach across their hatred and their rage to embrace each other in compassion and to share a meal. Regardless, within the city walls, the spear represented tyranny to the Athenians; and the sceptre represented hybris.

The alternative principle of government with which the Athenians experimented was that of public debate and open vote. Not only was each vote to be counted equally but each voice was to be heard with more or less equal openness to the possibility that it might express the truth. In case any individual citizen, even without claiming special authority or threatening the use of force, might attain a personal preeminence whose practical effect would be to intimidate others and to silence dissent, there was instituted the practice of ostracism, or temporary banishment. Ostracism, until it was debased, was a leveller, serving to eliminate for a time those individuals who were too gifted or too accomplished or too influential to take their place any longer as equals with their fellow citizens in common deliberation. It was, in a sense, a barbed tribute paid to genius. Under the democracy, the good of the city was to be found out in the process of searching for its common mind. The many were to become one, not through obedience to some higher authority, nor through fear of some greater force, nor through deference to some towering figure in their midst, but rather through coming together to a common mind and to a common voice. In this process there was no place for gods or demigods or brutes. Contrary to the animal sacrifices performed on the acropolis, the deliberations on the pnyx, which was the place of civic assembly, were purely human affairs. Just as the temple temenos marked off that area reserved for commerce with the sacred, so the assembly marked off that area reserved for indulgence in the profane consortium of men, reserved, we might say, for the free play of human passions and human wits.

By now we may well wonder what light this discursus into Athenian civics and city-planning could cast on the theatre. The point, however, which can be pressed home now is that, in the scheme of Athenian public life, theatre occupied a uniquely balanced position between the sacred rituals of the acropolis and the secular wrangles of the assembly. Athough in saying this I do not have in mind the theatre's literal, physical location, even in this respect the

35

ambiguity of the theatre was perhaps reflected; for the theatre of Dionysus, mounting as it does a steep slope of the acropolis, might well be seen as a bridge between the heights and the commons, between the timeless protocols of the gods and the urgencies of the all-too-human moment. The theatre of Dionysus indecisively spanned the *hiera*, the sacred, and the *hosia*, the profane. It was a place of sacrifice and cult, while at the same time it was a place wherein doubt, blasphemy, rage, and evil were hurled into open sight. It was a space reserved equally for pious and for impious words, for prayers and for curses.

The ambiguous character of the Athenian theatre ran far deeper, however, than we have yet explored here. After all, ancient theatre or, more specifically for our present purposes, tragic drama was an oral performance emergent from and controlled by a written text, and as such drew both from the oral poetic tradition and from the literary-critical tradition. Since the written text of a tragedy preceded and survived intact each rehearsal and each performance, it could be open with impunity to experimentation and criticism. Furthermore, since the written text was permanently present to prompt the actor's memory, the playwright was free to disregard the limitations of oral memory as well as any accompanying reliance on formulaic patterns and rhythms and to employ, instead, a diversity of meters and a complexity of language not possible in purely oral poetic composition and performance.

As in form, so also in content, the playwright drank from two streams. By convention, tragedy drew predominantly upon the poetic tradition for its *mythoi* or plots. Even in doing so, however, it was free to alter the myths at will, perhaps as a botanist may take cuttings from the oldest and most familiar plants to create something new and boldly different or as a photographer, though working in the most literal of all art forms, may enter the dark room and work creative wonders with the manipulation of light. Thus, in the *Helen*, Euripides, taking cuttings, as it were, from Homer, Herodotus, and Stesichorus, creates a delightfully novel hybrid-Helen, more like the faithful, pining Penelope than the whore of Hellas, while in the *Electra* he casts a more intense, inwardly revealing light on the otherwise quite recognizable princess and discloses a sexually stunted and obsessed adolescent, as enraged by her inadequate wardrobe as she is by her mother's murderous treason. In short, the ancient myths roused or provoked tragedy without determining its response. What this made possible was a public debate with the past, a visible, audible *agon* or struggle between all that was conscious and all that was unconscious in the Athenian psyche.

What may not at first glance be evident here is the freedom and the power bestowed on the playwright, on the one hand, by his inheritance of the entire mythic tradition of his race and, on the other hand, by the license accorded him to work whatever transformations he may wish upon that tradition. After all, the ancient myths and legends comprised the text from which Greeks learned to speak and to think; a mostly unwritten text, to be sure, but all the more compelling and inescapable for that fact. Learning one's mother tongue from stories, a coherent cosmos of stories woven with familiar images and rhythms, is barely to be compared with learning to speak and to think from texts which systematically present the elements and rules of phonetics and grammar. Language learned as a personal tool is well-suited to self-expression but is unlikely to create deep bonds with the past or the fellowship of shared imagination. The original difference here may be likened to that between breastfeeding and the intravenous infusion of a dietetically correct formula; and the eventual difference might perhaps be witnessed by contrasting the impeccably minced discourse of the university with the unstrained effusion of the bard who tilts back his head and drinks words as if they were the sweetest syrup. Words webbed in stories are not the same as words arranged alphabetically in vocabularly lists and indentified by mostly inept synonyms. Free-running words, like free-running chickens, truly do possess a different taste. But the heart of the matter here is not words but stories and images; and the point I wish to make is that Euripides, as an Athenian playwright, received as his legacy those stories and images which he knew were precisely those in the presence of which his audience's minds and hearts had first opened to their world.

Euripides, moreover, as playwright, possessed not only the power of the traditional stories but also power over them. Through major or minor alterations in plot, discourse, or tone, the playwright was able to create a split image, as it were. With the ancient image in mind and the new image before the eye, the spectator was confronted with a conflict between the received tradition and the present reality. Often, in the crevasse created between these two conflicting images, the Athenian public were invited, even forced, to contemplate themselves and their city and the contradictions which they were living.

When, for instance, the most celebrated and beloved of all the Greek heroes, Heracles, made his appearance in Euripides' *Heracles*, he suffered a rather critical loss of stature. This was in the mind of most Greeks the ancient "superman," whose brawn and bravado spawned cycles of legends in which he seemingly tamed all that was wild in the world save himself. In wresting power from beasts and women - achievements coveted and claimed by Athenians on behalf of Theseus, their own would-be Heracles - he made himself the titular founder and defender of Athenian patriarchy. In short, he was not a man to spend much time at home with the family or to betray the slightest weakness. The Euripidean Heracles, however, longed for nothing so much as a quiet life at home. He said farewell to his labors and confessed that he had been all wrong to have preferred them to the joys of family. He was by this time, however, a thoroughly violent man and violence has a way of spilling over, with or without daimonic intervention. Just as, in the Euripidean account, Orestes' furies roost within him, so the Euripidean Heracles comes to realize that he is the source and the object of his greatest labor, the most savage force he will ever confront. In a matter of minutes the man who had stood taller than any other man in the ancient imagination is broken, like a match. In the theatrical hands of Euripides, even Heracles, to say nothing of the Athenian spectators, has difficulty recognizing himself as he awakens from his mad slaughter. He thinks at first that his mind is clearing from one of his heroic labors, but like Agave in the *Bacchae*, what awaits him is not myth but reality. "I'm confused... ," he mutters as his wits return. "Where could I ever be helpless?" [1105] he wonders. This is certainly a question to which the tradition supplies no answer. He notices next that his father is weeping and he wonders what possible cause his father could have for tears. His father's response is simply: "even a god would weep if he knew what I know." [1115]

What, we may ask, did Amphitryon know? In a word, Amphitryon knew the truth; and so, by this time, did the Athenian theatre-goer. But these are not precisely the same truth. Amphitryon knew the truth of Heracles. He had witnessed with his own eyes his son turned, or rather revealed as, savage beast. The

38

Athenian public, however, knew, whether they accepted it or not, the truth of Athens; for they had witnessed the city of Theseus reveal in recent years its savage, slaughterous spirit. Athens, like Heracles, whose revered, received image was one of self-forgetful boldness and courage on behalf of Greek civilization, had for all its astounding accomplishments violated the first law of humanity, the lowest common denominator of human decency: "every race of man loves the lives it brings into the world." [636] Not so Athens, however, which had sent off its sons to die and to kill for nothing. For all the difference it made, Athens might as well have killed them itself.

It is not a great distance in the Greek imagination from Heracles to Athens. From the mythical Heracles to the legendary Theseus to the historical Athens there is a worn, familiar path, just as there is a virtually paved road from the seige of Troy or the siege of Thebes to the Persian Wars to the Peloponnesian War. Thus, when Euripidies demythologizes, as it were, the glories of the mythic past, revealing the siege of Troy as a deranged misadventure, the violent orgasmic phantasy of a rabble chiefed not by noble lords but by callous non-entities, the mercilessly revealing light cast on the remote past falls on the more recent past, as well, and threatens more immediate myths with reality. Myth, legend, history, and present reality in the Greek theatre are like layers of skin. They do not peel away one at a time, painlessly, like filo dough. When Euripides offered to the Athenian public, for instance, the *Trojan Women*, he was not distracting or entertaining them any more than Medea intended to delight Jason's bride with her gifts. Words like the following [*Trojan Women*,1158-1160], though literally provoked by the murder of Astyanax and spoken by Hecuba to Talthybius, must have been no easier to remove than Medea's gown, once Euripides had hurled them out at the same citizens who, assembled on the pnyx, had only recently called for the senseless massacre and demolition of Melos:

> Achaeans! You know how to hurl a spear; but
> not how to use your mind or your heart.
> What was it about this little child that
> made you so afraid that you had to kill him,
> and go about it so savagely?

39

In short, Athens' mythic icons were at the same time mirrors; and any alteration or distortion in the images of the past reflected immediately upon the present. Thus when Euripides exposed the traditional Olympian pantheon as a household wherein the most callous, petty, selfish, cowardly, vindictive, jealous, and cruel behavior was commonplace and at the same time presented the great lords of legend as chips off the divine block, he left the Athenians with little of stature in terms of which to flatter and defend themselves. He gave them a mythology reduced to scale, a debased mythology suited to a debased city. "Human nature," wrote T.S. Eliot, "is able to endure only a little reality." If this is true, then Euripides brought the Athenians to the edge of endurance.

It is not surprising that Euripides was accused of having denigrated the tragic tradition. Tragedy implies stature and in a great many of Euripides' plays the traditionally central figures are too small in everything but their pain to command a tragic response. Empires and the mythologies which accompany them display a penchant for grandeur; and this is precisely what Euripides denied his fellow citizens. His were dark times and he offered a vision suitable for eyes accomodated to darkness. In the search for human excellence, Euripides overlooked the seats of traditional privilege and directed the eye, instead, to the traditionally least likely places, to the margins of human existence. As we shall see later in some detail, it was to women, slaves, peasants, barbarians, the very old and the very young, all those excluded from canonical heroism, if not from humanity, that Euripides turned to display new, unconventional paradigms of nobility. Euripides overturned the traditional hierarchy premised on privilege, stood it on end, in fact.

The most privileged, of course, were the gods, whose exemption from death made them all the more unfeeling and unaccountable in their exercise of power. Next were the kings and princes, whose relative exemption from suffering and whose disproportionate power enabled them briefly to live and think as if they were gods. At the base of this traditional pyramid of privilege and power were those whose weakness and vulnerability left them to suffer without recourse, without respite. By revealing the corruption that accompanies power and the wisdom that comes with suffering, Euripides endeavored to redefine heroism. As a rule, it was not those who suffered last and least, but rather those who suffered first

40

and most who stood tallest and shone forth on the Euripidean stage. Alcestis, Macaria, Iolaus, Polyxena, Theonoe and her slave, Menoeceus, Electra's peasant husband, and Iphigeneia, for example, tower over their husbands, fathers, kings, lords, and murderers, who command mostly our contempt.

By presenting its traditional ideals in moral disarray, Euripides fostered the radical critique of Athenian society; and by creating a new canon of heroism, he provided what might have been the first elements in a revisioning of that society. The Greek theatre, then, clearly made possible not only sight but insight. It was the choice of the playwright whether to question or to confirm the common vision and the common mind more or less fixed by tradition. It was indeed possible for the playwright to challenge directly the amalgam of myth, historical half-truth, prejudice, and delusion which formed the consensus of ordinary public opinion. Although steeped in myth, theatre was uniquely vulnerable to the incursions of historical reality. Although heir to the poetic tradition, tragedy unlike epic was each time a fresh creation written with a single performance in mind. Belonging to a particular moment as epic poetry never did, tragedy resonated as fully to the immediate present as to the mythic or indefinite past. In short, everything and nothing was sacred in the theatre, reflecting as it did both myth and history, the sacred and the profane, the received tradition and the present reality.

A further light is shed on the middle ground occupied by Greek theatre when Aristotle, in the *Poetics*, assigns poetry, and specifically dramatic poetry, to a middle place between philosophy and history. In distinguishing dramatic poetry from philosophy and history, Aristotle makes quite clear that the most obvious difference here - the fact that poetry is written in verse and both philosophy and history are not - falls wide of the point he wishes to make. History and philosophy could be written in verse and drama in prose without altering their respective natures, as Aristotle understands them. The key to this understanding lies not in the literary form but in the essential subject matter of each. History concerns itself with actual events, with what has happened rather than with what could or should happen. Poetry, on the other hand, is free of the actual course of events, free to consider whatever is possible. In short, history addresses particulars, while poetry addresses universals. It is for this reason that Aristotle says of poetry that it is more serious and

41

elevated, in fact more philosophical, than history. It is only fair to note here that Aristotle has in mind, as his paradigmatic historian, not Thucydides but Herodotus. It is not clear, in fact, that Aristotle knew at all the work of Thucydides, who is in Aristotle's categories as clearly a poet as he is a historian. Regardless, the distinction being made here between a concern with particulars and a concern with universals remains critically illuminating.

On the face of it, however, both tragic poets and historians are storytellers, the one admittedly less critical of his sources than the other. After all, the tragic poet's stories are mostly from the mythic past, to which no chain of human witnesses can be traced back. The historian, on the other hand, would have us believe that his stories, which relate more recent events, rest upon more reliable grounds, upon more or less trustworthy human memory and testimony. In short, it would seem that what divides the tragic poet from the historian comes down to time and its effects. And if this were truly the heart of the matter, we might say that the tragic poet is a teller of pre-historic stories, while the historian is a teller of historic stories. In saying this, we would miss Aristotle's point, however, which is that even though the stories of the theatre appear to be about particulars, namely, about individual persons and events, they truly are not. In other words, when Euripides tells a story of Theseus and when Herodotus tells a story of Themistocles, we miss the essential distinction between their accounts if we focus on our awareness that Theseus is a less historically stable individual, that is, a more fictional and less factual individual than is Themistocles, and in doing so never question their equal claim to individuality. In order to grasp what Aristotle is saying about tragic poetry, we must loosen our fixation on the distinction between fact and fiction and consider instead the distinction between fact and truth. This is made all the more difficult by the characteristically modern identification of fact and truth, an identification which cannot go unchallenged, however, if we are to approach Greek theatre with any perception.

When Aristotle says that dramatic poetry is philosophical because of its essential concern with universals, he is in effect saying that dramatic poetry is concerned with truth. We would perhaps argue that the historian is no less concerned with truth, with telling the true story, for example, of Themistocles. But Aristotle means something different by "truth" than we have in mind in arguing for the

42

legitimacy of historical truth-telling. Of course, any full account of Aristotle's understanding of truth falls well beyond the reasonable bounds of our present discussion. Nonetheless, we cannot hope for even a provisional grasp of the ancient playwright as teacher, nor of the ancient theatre as a seeing-place, nor of ancient dramatic poetry as philosophical without some brief venture into the conception of truth inherent in Aristotle's analysis of dramatic poetry.

In appealing here to Aristotle, I am not claiming that Aristotle's teaching shaped Euripidean drama; for to claim that I would have to turn back time itself. Rather, I am claiming that Aristotle was a well-informed and intelligent commentator on Attic tragedy, sufficiently close, both in time and in sensibility, to the fifth-century tragic playwrights to reveal in their work much that is all but lost on our less-knowing gaze. Further, I would argue that the few Aristotelian categories employed in my comments provide a usefully concise articulation of elements which can be shown to lie already within, indeed at the core of, Euripidean drama and, for that matter, of all Attic tragedy as we know it. Presumably, it was to his own similar perception of the convergence and congeniality of his work with that of the theatre that Aristotle was pointing when he called dramatic poetry "philosophical."

The truth whose meaning we are exploring here, the truth of theatre and of philosophy, is the truth of universals or universal truth. "Universal truth" and "universals," though the most common way of translating the relevant Greek words, are all too likely to mislead us here, however; for they have acquired too many contemporary connotations alien to our purposes. I say this because the "universal" of consummate concern in Euripidean theatre is humanity or human nature. Now, in contemporary usage, to speak of the universal truth of humanity or of human nature, is to speak of that which is true of all human beings, if indeed there is anything true of all human beings. The way we would determine whether some attribute or behavior were universally human, in the sense of universally true of human beings, would presumably be through the exhaustive observation of all individual human beings, which is, of course, not feasible. Consequently, we are left with approximations of the truth, which is to say that we are left with claims to the effect that every human being observed by us has displayed the particular attribute or behavior whose universality we would argue. Modern statistical theories and methods have provided plausible grounds for reaching and defending conclusions well beyond the scope of those individuals actually observed; but nothing can alter the essentially quantitative character of this conception of universality. The conception of universality central to, and even constitutive of, ancient theatre is not, however, essentially quantitative, but qualitative.

The truth of human nature, as it is sought out and revealed in Greek drama, is more appropriately described as that which is true **for** all human beings, rather than that which is true **of** all human beings. What this distinction permits us to acknowledge is that there are attributes and actions which are true **for** all human beings yet not true **of** all human beings. And if this is the case, mere observation is useless as a means for the discovery of universal truth. What is required, instead, is insight. And insight is the proper work and aim of the ancient theatre. Before burrowing even further into these reflections, however, a straightforward example from Euripides' *Alcestis* [779-784,787-788,799] may well serve to ground and to clarify the matter at hand. The voice we hear in the following lines is that of Heracles, drunken and rowdy, conducting his own private debauch in the mourning house of Admetus. He addresses the household servant who is supplying him with wine and feast.

> You there, c'mere.
> I'm gonna make you a wiser man.
> Do you know what's what?
> I mean do you know what it means to be human?
> I don't think you do.
> Anyway, you listen to me.
> We all gotta die.
> There ain't one of us alive today
> That knows whether he'll be around tomorrow...
> So there, that's it.
> You heard what I got to teach.
> Enjoy yourself, have a drink...
> If you're mortal,
> You gotta have mortal thoughts.

44

The braying Heracles, of course, his tongue loosened with wine, had more than this to say; but I've preserved the core of his teaching. Essentially it comes down to this: all human beings die and they ought to live and think as if they know it. What we may notice about his teaching is that one of its tenets is true **of** all human beings. It is true of all human beings that they "gotta die." The second teaching, he would claim, is true **for** all human beings but is surely not true **of** all or even most. It is true for all human beings that they "gotta have mortal thoughts." Both death and the consciousness of death are prescribed. Both belong to the nature of human beings. Both are universally true. But the truth and necessity of the one must be distinquished from the truth and necessity of the other. The one we may call a literal necessity and the other a moral necessity. The one describes what it is to be mortal and the other describes what it ought to mean to be mortal. What we notice next is the relationship between these two universal truths or necessities. It is the literal truth that enjoins the moral truth. It is because we are mortal that we ought to think and to act as if we are mortal. In other words, we must, in the sense of should, live in accord with our nature.

Clearly it is the possibility of living in violation of one's nature that accounts for the fact that what is morally true for all is not actually true of them. All human beings ought to think mortal thoughts and to act accordingly; but not all do. Heracles prefaced his remarks, we remember, with the claim that what he had to say was going to make a wiser man of the servant. Presumably, Heracles' first teaching was not news to the servant, who is noticeably distressed over the death of Alcestis. That we all "gotta die" is a truism, lost only on the youngest children. But few are those, as Camus once wrote, who pursue life's truisms to their final conclusions. It is not the literal knowledge of death's inevitability that makes anyone appreciably wiser, but rather the reasonings and resolves which ought to accompany, but most often do not accompany, that knowledge.

The path of wisdom, then, requires that facts be transformed into truths, that truisms be pursued until they yield their moral conclusions. Euripides, as a teacher of his city, is engaged precisely in this endeavor. Not unlike Heracles, Euripides is concerned to make a wiser man out of whoever listens to him. No doubt such a concern rings rather pretentiously, even offensively, in many or most modern ears. After all, modern theatre is there, it would seem, to

45

entertain, not to edify.   We underestimate and trivialize ancient theatre, however, if we overlook what Aristotle called its more serious, elevated, even philosophical nature. The ancient theatre is a seeing-place, a place avowedly consecrated to communal moral insight, a place where light is shed upon universal necessities and truths, those moral necessities and truths which hold for all human beings, however widely they ignore and defy them.

The tragic theatre, in sum, is a place of disclosure, a place of truth. Even the Greek word for truth - *aletheia* - gives us privileged entry into the ideas to be explored here. *Aletheia* literally means that which has not escaped notice, that which has not gone unseen, or that which has not been forgotten. What this derivation seems to suggest is that truth, unless ferreted out and grasped tightly, is likely to slip away, once discovered, or to elude us altogether. Truth, conceived as "unconcealment," presupposes concealment as the raw condition of truth. It is as if truth, like precious metal, must be mined, extracted, as it were, from darkness.   "Nature," said Heraclitus, "likes to hide," which is not far from our present point, inasmuch as the truth of central concern to Euripides is that of human nature. Perhaps it is also the case that human nature likes to hide and is likely to elude us unless it is dragged into open view and unless we, in turn, are coaxed into confronting it. One place wherein both occur, I would propose, is the ancient theatre.

In another equally enticing aphorism, Heraclitus points out how, when we dream, we inhabit a private world. When we awake, however, he says we awake to a common world. Here again we find a metaphor for truth and its disclosure. Truth is common; and to behold it each individual must be roused from private dreams to public vision. It is not only that when we dream we dwell in a private world, but also that when we dwell in a private world we are only dreaming. The city is ideally a place where humanity flourishes; and humanity is common, universal, as an obligation if not as an achievement. Therefore, when the city, guided by the playwright's counsel, is brought to a common vision, that vision is first and essentially the vision of humanity, lured out of concealment into the common light of day and into the shared light of reason to be contemplated and embraced.

How, we might ask, does this awakening occur? How is a common vision achieved? In the most preliminary and literal sense, the city is led to a common vision by being collected in the theatre and presented with a common spectacle. By vision, however, we mean more than this. We mean insight; for only through shared insight does a community form a common mind. The stories enacted in the Athenian theatre, like the fables of Aesop, are transparent to *logos*, to thought and idea. In the case of Aesop, the *logos* - usually translated as the "moral" - yielded by each fable is explicitly stated and more often than not represents a commonplace of folk wisdom. In the case of Euripides, however, the *logos* embedded in each drama is more complex and less explicit. The moral issues explored in Euripidean drama rarely admit of direct, univocal declarations. Instead, we are presented with a dilemma and a debate. There are multiple lines of force, as we shall see, in the Euripidean theatre; and, for every line of force, a voice to argue its case. The outcome, while not simplistically didactic, is far from cacophony. The playwright's voice is discernible, even though it is fractured and filtered through his characters, like light refracted through a crystal; for there is an order, a scheme, in Euripidean theatre which rendered his drama not only visible but intelligible to its original spectators. For the most part that order is visual and thus spatial; and is prior to any words spoken. In Greek theatre, the visual order frames and provides the interpretive structure for the many voices woven together in the text. The remainder of this chapter, and in fact the remainder of this book, will address that visual order and the insight it made possible.

It has already been claimed, while discussing dramatic poetry's philosophical concern with universal truth, that the stories or *mythoi* unfolded in the tragic theatre are not truly about individuals. This fact would have been more evident to ancient Athenian spectators than to ourselves, both because they **saw** Greek theatre and because what they saw outwardly in the theatre corresponded to and confirmed, in its most essential structure, the categories of their most inward thoughts. In a word, what I am pointing to here is the fact and the significance of the fact that ancient tragedy was **masked**. On the face of it this is no startling revelation. Everyone knows that Greek tragedy, and all of Greek drama for that matter, was performed with masks. Whatever other ancient theatrical conventions were challenged and adapted or abandoned, all classical Greek theatre was masked. It might be argued that masks were dictated by merely practical considerations. How were men to play credibly the parts of

47

women, for example, without wearing masks? And how could the three actors, to whom the playwright was conventionally limited, have played more than three characters without the ready changes of identity made possible by masks? There may well be answers to these questions; but we need not quarrel with the obvious utility of masks. It is not for their utility, however, that they were adopted; for the use of masks in ritual and drama, both in ancient Greece and elsewhere, precedes and oversteps the specific conventions of classical theatre which one might otherwise imagine to have dictated that use. Besides, what I have in mind by saying that Greek theatre was masked extends well beyond the literal use of painted cloth coverings for head and face.

To say that Greek theatre was masked is to say that in Greek theatre personal identities were concealed. The closest Greek word to "personal identity" or "personality" is *prosopon*, which curiously is the word both for face and for mask. *Prosopon* means that which is looked upon, that aspect of a human being which is most visible. It is, we could say, one's visible identity. This makes evident sense, for though one may be visually identified by one's stature, or physique, by one's hands or feet or walk, it is by one's face that one is, as we say, "positively identified". To cover the face is to make one invisible, in the sense of unidentifiable. What I wish to claim in all this is that the essential function of Greek theatrical masks was not only to conceal the identity of the actor but to conceal personal identity altogether and to bestow upon the masked character a universal significance instead of an alternative personality.

Both to stress the fact that, in exploring the masked character of Greek theatre, I have something more in mind than the physical mask, as well as to illuminate what this "something more" might be, I will point to another ancient masked ritual in which no physical masks were used. This was the ritual of hospitality, which constituted one of the most sacred moral obligations in ancient Greece, under the direct patronage of Zeus himself, who was thought to take the punishment of offenders into his own hands. The aspect of this ritual which is of critical interest here is the anonymity customarily imposed upon those who make the ritual request of hospitality. The Greek word both for guest and for host is *xenos* or stranger; for host and guest are to be and to remain strangers to each other in the requesting, the giving, and the receiving of hospitality. Not until the pledge of

4 8

hospitality has been made and accepted, in fact not until the stranger-host has provided the stranger-guest with a room, a bath, a fresh robe, and a first meal, which is to say not until the bond between host and guest has been sealed, is the guest to reveal his indentity. Before that moment he is a stranger.

This strange behavior has a brilliant truth at its core. If the guest's identity is known, the extending or withholding of hospitality may well be influenced by that knowledge. The host may discover that he is related to the guest or that they both come from the same town or that the guest is related to an enemy or is from a part of the world for which the host has nothing but contempt. Whatever the host finds out about the guest's individuality may influence and complicate the way he sees the man before him. And any such influences and complications are irrelevant to the obligation of hospitality, which is due to any other human being in need of a roof and a meal. The bond of hospitality is to be a bond between human beings, rooted in the recognition of a common humanity, not in the discovery of shared idiosyncrasies. What is displayed in the giving and receiving of hospitality is not the unique regard one individual has for another but the essential good-will assumed to exist in the heart of any human being for another. The initial silence of the guest regarding his identity is a mask worn over his individuality. The function of this mask is, however, not only to conceal a reality but also to reveal one. The revealed reality is the guest's humanity, which is ordinarily masked by his individuality. Kings, slaves, employers, cousins, welfare recipients, and AIDS victims, citing several possible indentities at random, are less likely to be seen simply and straightforwardly in their humanity once their particulars are known. Personal familiarity conspires to estrange individuals from their common humanity, just as the shared ritual estrangement of host and guest serves to reconcile them to their common humanity. By now the point I wish to make is doubtlessly clear. Ancient Greek theatre was a masked ritual in precisely the same sense as was the ritual of hospitality, and with the same end in mind: to reveal the essential commonality of all its participants and to revive among them the essential good-will and mutuality without which human community is an idle phantasy.

The anonymity imposed upon Greek theatre is, to be sure, in no way as total as that proper to the rites of hospitality. In the theatre, the human mask is admittedly particularized, and comes in many forms. Each mask, however, as it conceals the identity of the actor and receives the identity of a specific character in the plot, remains open to and reveals the wider, more embracing, generic category to which that character belongs. In Attic drama, each character is visibly defined and positioned within two fundamental orders, which I will call **the metaphysical order** and **the political order**. Within the metaphysical order, the three essentially distinct spheres of being are those of gods, humans, and beasts. The focus of tragedy invariably falls upon the human sphere; for both gods and beasts are spared, or perhaps we should say denied, mortal poignancy. Human consciousness must define itself against the distorting irrelevancies of divine and bestial existence; and tragic consciousness is nothing if it is not human consciousness brought to brightest flame. The second order, the political order, lies wholly within the human sphere and comprises all of those distinctions between human beings which sever them one from the other and may appear to constitute essential differences between them. In the political order, men are distinguished from women, citizens from slaves, Greeks from barbarians, the rich from the poor, the young from the old, and so on. Both orders, as understood within those archaic conventions inherited by Euripides, constituted hierarchies of privilege and power. Within the immutable metaphysical order, gods were the masters of mortals, and mortals were the masters of beasts, while within the altogether mutable political order, the balance of power slides and shifts, as Hecuba reminds Odysseus [*Hecuba,*282-284]:

> The powerful do not do well
>   to abuse their power.
> No turn of fate fails to turn some day.
> I know.
> I was once where you are now.
> You see how much remains.

Each character's place within these two orders is made visibly evident on the ancient tragic stage, not only by the mask that is worn but by other semiotic conventions, as well. The human visage is unmistakeable, but in itself is possibly misleading; for gods often take human form. If we realize that the tragic stage was itself vertically

50

divided into metaphysical spheres, then the place of each character within that most fundamental order becomes more apparent. Too removed from the human condition to feel its pain and too near to resist meddling, the gods drift over the human realm suspended from the "machine" or stand aloof atop the stage building. They speak down to mortals, while mortals speak up to the gods. The more that the gods flaunt their divinity and the more that wretched mortals acknowledge it, the greater becomes the visible gulf dividing them. Thus, in the face of manifest divinity, mortals fall to their knees or prostrate themselves flat upon the earth, not even raising their eyes. In such moments, the identity of the mortal, or that of the divinity, for that matter, is beside the point. What is seen is the otherness, the sheer immeasurable power and preeminence of gods and, by contrast, the abject helplessness of mortals. Thus, for example, in the *Electra*, the *Helen*, the *Iphigeneia in Tauris*, or the *Orestes*, when one or other of the gods veers in on the machine to decree what is to be, there can be no question of human resistance to the divine will. What is revealed, when gods and mortals clash, is not finally a conflict of wills or personalities but an inescapable conflict of natures. Gods and mortals are fated by the radical incompatibitity of their natures to misunderstand each other and would be wrong to take their differences personally, as we too would be wrong to interpret them so.

Similarly, within the political or inter-human order, masks, costumes, stage position, posture, and gesture all conspire to make visibly evident the peculiar station of each character, as well as the relative power or weakness concomitant with that station. Youth and age, for example, are immediately visible on the ancient tragic stage. A boy has no beard, a mature man a dark beard, and an old man a white or grey beard. A modern reader or spectator of an ancient drama might be inclined to overlook or to underestimate the critical significance of these and other such categorical differentiations which serve to reveal its political design, the lines of force motive within it. In the *Alcestis*, to cite one instance, the fierce confrontation between Admetus and Pheres is less likely to be seen as the collision of two colossal egotists, if Admetus' callow youth and Pheres' cantankerous seniority are noted and given their due. Even more crucially, in the *Bacchae*, the brittle arrogance, the conflicted voyeurism, the rigid prurience of Pentheus are all made coherent and

51

sympathetically intelligible by the recognition of his adolescence, a fact which would have been immediately visible to any original spectator but which we must learn in the last moments of the play from a chance reference to what we call "peach fuzz" on his severed head. In the same way, whether a woman was young or old, married, unmarried or widowed was clear for all to see from the moment of her entry. Kings are known perhaps from crowns or from their elevated stage positions or from the fact that others bow or fall to their knees before them. Barbarians too are unmistakable, as are slaves. The entrances of characters into the Greek theatre represent at the same time the entrances of realities, natures, forces, and ideas which shadow in importance the individual character who happens to convey them there. Aristotle could not be more clear or correct on this: that Athenian tragedy is not about individual character. Rather, it is about that action into which one is propelled by forces active without and within the individual and which are beyond the individual to limit and control. It is about nature and fate, which Heraclitus aphoristically fuses together and which could not be entwined more tightly than they are on the Euripidean stage.

In Euripidean drama, individuals are prey to their metaphysical and political natures. Gods and mortals are destined either to collide or to pass indifferently in the night, but never to know commonality or friendship. And those humans whose disproportionate privileges or deprivations, power or weakness divide them from each other, as if they were radically diverse beings, must summon nearly incomprehensible will and insight to recognize their common humanity and to embrace in fellowship. More commonly, the political order mirrors and mimics the metaphysical order. Human beings lord it over each other, playing out their power and yielding to their weakness as their respective necessities demand of them. Some act as if they were gods while others, in turn, are treated as if they were beasts.

In sum, these two orders, the metaphysical and the political, describe the essential scope and structure of the Greek theatre. They are the templates for the curriculum which Euripides, as playwright and teacher, brought to vision in the Athenian theatre. They are the templates, as well, for all that follows in this particular endeavor to approach the sight and the insight still residing in Euripidean drama.

III. THE METAPHYSICAL ORDER

The claim which has brought us to this point in our discussion is that the Athenian tragic theatre, and in particular the theatre of Euripides, had as its defining endeavor the disclosure of human nature. In this context, it has been suggested that human nature, as discerned by the ancient Greeks, is inclined towards concealment and must be brought to light and to open view, if it is to be seen by all. This work, the proper work of the Athenian playwright, of bringing to light human being may be understood as a clarification or definition of human being; for the wonted concealment of human being is most often a matter of its confusion with other beings. And insofar as the aim of this work, though not necessarily its method, is philosophical, the classical Greek philosophers are singularly clear-sighted and articulate guides in our efforts to grasp what is meant by defining the nature of human being, which is why we turn initially to the writings of Plato and Aristotle for our preliminary orientation.

In the *Phaedo* [96a6-10], Socrates says that he too was eager to be wise, in the sense of being able to give an account of the nature of things. He goes on to say that it seemed to him a resplendent achievement to have seen the origins or causes of each thing, which is to have seen why each thing comes into being, why it passes out of being, and why it is what it is. Elsewhere, in the *Phaedrus* [230a1-6], Socrates admits that he is rather single-mindedly concerned to be able to give an account of human nature; for he confesses that, until he knows the truth of human being, i.e. the truth of his own being, he finds it rather ludicrous to pursue an understanding of other truths and other natures. In short, he says he has no time for these. It is the human question that interests him, the question of human being, which he formulates in the following manner. He wonders whether he is, as a human being, some bestial being in the savage order of a Typhon or rather a living being with some more gentle and civilized nature. He recognizes that individual human beings can aspire to either extreme possibility, that they may become in practice either the most sublime beings on earth or the most savage. Both are equally available; but they are not equally appropriate. What decides the appropriateness or inappropriateness of these possibilities is the truth of human nature, which Euripides, no less than Socrates, seeks.

Aristotle, in fact, begins his *Metaphysics* [280a22-28] with insights which have direct bearing on our present discussion. He says that all human beings by nature desire to know, which he immediately links to the special delight we take in seeing. Sight, more than any other of the senses, explains Aristotle, leads us to understanding and reveals to us the differences between things. When we see the differences between things, we see these things for what they truly are, without confusion. To have seen something in this way, clearly and distinctly, is to know it. This very confidence is embedded in the Greek language itself; for the word for "I know" [*oida*] means literally "I have seen." To know the nature or the truth of human being, then, is to have seen its coming into being and its passing out of being, and to have seen it for what it is, apart from what it is not. In short, to know human being is to have seen it "defined" or "in definition," which, as the etymology of this word suggests, is to have seen the limits of human being.

In order to remind ourselves that these questions are not foreign to Euripides, but in fact lie at the center of his concerns, we may recall the paedogogical confrontation between Dionysus and Pentheus in the *Bacchae*, "paedogogical" because Dionysus comes to Thebes essentially as a teacher, a teacher from the "old school" we might say. "Whether it wants to or not," threatens Dionysus, "this city must learn its lesson." [39] Some of the citizens, indeed, are quick to learn the lesson, as two of these, Teiresias and Cadmus, make clear when they boast that they alone have seen the light. The lesson, it seems, comes down to this: the discernment and acknowledgment of one's humanity. Cadmus sums it up when he says: "I am mortal. I don't aspire to the gods, nor do I disdain them." [199] Dionysus, speaking for himself, says from the outset that he has come and taught his dances and mysteries with one end in mind: that he might be utterly manifest [*emphanes*] to human beings as the god that he is. These two events - the theophany of Dionysus and the human insight of Cadmus - are appropriately bonded together. When a god manifests himself in his divinity, it highlights not only divinity but humanity; for the gulf between human nature and divine nature yawns open in the process. Somehow, Pentheus clings to his folly in the face of Dionysus' instructive disclosures of his divinity, a folly which Dionysus sums up and flings back at Pentheus in these words [506]:

> You don't know [literally: you have not seen]
>   why you are alive,
>   what you are doing,
>   or who you are.

Pentheus is a fool because he fails to learn or to acknowledge his limits; not his personal limits, but the limits of his human nature. He has no sense of where he begins or where he leaves off. He would deny his roots in the bestial and imagine his equivalence to the divine. These, after all, are the borders of the human, borders on which human folly is prone to trespass. To see the human "in definition" without confusion is to see humanity as distinct both from bestiality and from divinity. This vision corresponds directly to that of the city, the *polis*; for the city is that place designed and reserved for human beings. As Aristotle puts it, in the *Politics* [1253a], "anyone who proves incapable of human collaboration or who is so self-sufficient as to stand in no need of others, has no share in the city, like a beast or a god." Clearly, the definition of human being and the definition of the human realm, namely the polis, coincide in the theatre where both are imaginatively envisioned for the edification and politicization of all citizens.

If we are to understand the ancient significance and urgency of defining human being and the human realm, we must realize the ambiguity with which they were once surrounded and pervaded. Human nature, as imagined in poetry, portrayed in art, and reasoned over in philosophical and scientific discussions, was seen by the ancient Greeks as poised unstably between two extreme and foreign natures, that of beasts and that of gods. The relationship between the human realm and these two inhuman realms was a matter of profound uncertainty and nearly obsessive concern. Mid-way

55

between beasts and gods, humanity was at once the battlezone wherein radically antithetical forces confronted each other and itself an unhappy synthesis of the most fundamental cosmological categories. Humanity was at once descended and estranged from the beasts, while at the same time aspirant and hostile to the gods.

In case this idea of fundamental metaphysical ambiguity might seem to a modern reader to be a quite bizarre and benighted preoccupation, I would point to a similar preoccupation closer to home as we know it. While the modern secular critique of religion has removed from many minds any concern over the imminence of divine being, and while the modern natural and behavioral sciences have removed any conviction of an essential divide between human beings and animals, a rather new and curious metaphysical ambiguity has surfaced both in scientific discussion and in popular imagination. This recently emergent ambiguity is that between man and the man-made, between human being and artefact. In formal terms, I refer to research in artificial intelligence, bionics, and robotics; but of more immediate interest is the contemporary spillover of science into popular culture, where a genuine confusion exists between man and machine. The media are by now so infiltrated with androids that certainty no longer exists from one moment to the next whether the character who has evoked our sympathy, rage, admiration or amour is composed of sinew and soul like "us" or is, instead, composed of microchips and printed circuitry. More important, however, is the increasing sensibility which suggests that it doesn't truly matter one way or the other. Even the saving remnant who would argue that there is some essential difference between human and artificial being, most often find themselves at a loss to articulate convincingly the decisive difference between what is "natural" and what is "artificial" and are at an even greater loss to mount a compelling case for preferring the natural over against the artificial.

I have no intention of belaboring this issue here; for my only point is that pervasive cultural confusion and debate over the metaphysical status of human being have only changed their focus rather than slipped into extinction. The "human question" of Socrates remains a border dispute; but today's disputed border is a different one from those under scrutiny in ancient Greece. For the ancient Greeks, as for the entire ancient East Mediterranean world, the ambiguous boundaries requiring clarification were those we have already noted - the boundaries between humans, beasts, and gods - and to which we now turn.

Volumes could and have been written on the theme which we now set out to explore and which we can do no more than sketch. In our effort to glimpse and to grasp the ancient understanding of metaphysical ambiguity, we will turn first to visual art, then to poetry, and finally to philosophical and scientific speculation. Firstly, it is clear that no more telling evidence of ancient metaphysical ambiguity may be offered than ancient Greek, Egyptian, and Near Eastern visual art, which abounds in fantastic hybrids of all three metaphysical categories: gods in part-human, part-bestial forms, men that are part-beasts or beasts that are part-men, and so on. In some instances, these hybrids seem relatively stable, while in other instances they undergo frequent, unpredictable transmutations. What is manifest in all instances is the fact that ambiguity was a primary cosmological element in the ancient East Mediterranean world.

Gorgons and satyrs seem to have been among the first such hybrids to take root and to achieve prominence in the Greek imagination, and by the late Geometric period a plethora of oriental hybrid beings had entered Greek art: sphinxes, centaurs, chimaeras, and boreads, to name a few. Long before the seventh and sixth centuries, in which fantastic bestiaries flourished in Greek art, composite beings had been already common in Minoan and Mycenaean art. In interpreting this phenomenon, however, we are left with our conjectures, since neither the Greeks nor their neighbors explained their iconographic fascination with the mingling of diverse natures. If intuitions have any standing at all in these matters, however, it seems unlikely that anyone gazing with any duration and thoughtfulness at ancient East Mediterranean gods and monsters will fail to sense the awful otherness of these beings and yet their kinship with our fears and fascinations and desires. However these peoples must have seen and thought about gods and beasts, they must have seen them as **other**, inaccessible in their beauty, wisdom, power, courage, cunning, and grace, and yet as somehow bonded to the human by virtue of human sympathy, imagination, and desire. In saying even this, we are perhaps saying both too much and too little, when the art is already eloquent on its own behalf. Surely it leaves us with a feeling that the divine, the human, and the bestial are set apart from each other by a great divide and yet are one.

Turning now to poetry, we find that the oldest and most widely diffused tale in the ancient Near East, the epic of Gilgamesh, had as its central theme the definition and quest of human being as distinct from divine and bestial being. This tale, however difficult its influences on Greek literature may be to trace directly, doubtlessly affected Greek poetic imagination as deeply as Near Eastern sculpture and painting affected Greek visual art. Its two heroes, Gilgamesh and Enkidu, may be described as frontiersmen in the ancient endeavor to define the specifically human realm, its appropriate aspirations and necessities. At the outset of the tale, Gilgamesh is described as a man who is two-thirds divine and yet wild like a bull. Enkidu, on the other hand, begins at the other end of the metaphysical spectrum. With a gazelle for a mother and a wild ass as a father and raised by creatures with tails, Enkidu is a man who, it is written, is two-thirds beast and yet likened to the gods. In short, in these two characters we encounter metaphysical ambiguity with a vengeance. The poem describes the slow, excruciating process of their mutual humanization. It is the story of their becoming human together.

Without losing ourselves in this wondrous tale, we must note that in it the human touchstone is mortality. No matter how intimately Gilgamesh and Enkidu may have mingled with gods and beasts, no matter how hybrid their natures, they are finally defined by their mortality. It is of no ultimate consequence that they are two-thirds divine or two-thirds bestial. A one-third portion of humanity, or even less, suffices to condemn one to mortality; and from mortality all else that is human follows. "Even the sons of the gods," writes Euripides in the *Alcestis* [989-990], "go dark in death," which might as well be a line from the *Gilgamesh*. Gilgamesh, "he who knew everything," is also described as "the man who saw the abyss." With his companion Enkidu, Gilgamesh hunted the beast-favorites of the gods, rejected *hierogamy* or sacred union with a goddess, and, most decisively, watched his friend, his other self, die in his arms. In that moment, he says, sorrow came into his belly and death took up habitation in his bed, in his house, companioned him everywhere he went. In time he relinquishes his inward evasions and outward quests for any release from the truth he has come to know, and accepts the essential human truth of mortality, which brings him back to his home, to the towering, familiar walls of his city.

58

Greek poetry could not be more resonant with the quests and truths pioneered by Gilgamesh and Enkidu. That mortality is the defining truth of human being and the source of undeluded human consciousness is altogether central to the poetry of Homer as well as to that of Euripides. In fact, the friendship of Gilgamesh and Enkidu, which leaps like a flame from their mutual collision with mortality, may be seen as the prototype for the friendship of Achilles and Patroclus; and the idea of *ibru* or friendship manifest in the Gilgamesh text is intriguingly close to the idea of *philia* or friendship so effulgent in the *Iliad* and so pervasive in the plays of Euripides. Beyond Achilles, who like Gilgamesh is part-human and part-divine and likened to a beast, Greek literature abounds in hybrid beings. The forms and circumstances of these various beings and their metamorphoses are at once too numerous and too notorious to require any cataloguing here. Always, however, what remains decisive for humanity is the necessity of death and the consciousness which wells up from that necessity. It is this keen-edged truth and the clarity it brings with it that makes possible in drama the sorting out of essential confusions.

This same metaphysical ambiguity and confusion found frequent voice in ancient Greek scientific and philosophical speculation. Both in Greece and in the Near East there was from the earliest times a belief that in the beginning, or before the beginning, all things were fused and formless. Various theories were proposed to give a coherent account of the emergence of differentiation and order; but behind this order there lay primordial unity. More often than not, the sorting out or separation of things is neither thorough or final. Thus Anaxagoras [fr.11] suggests that "in everything there is a share of everything else, except for Mind [*nous*]." Some things, in his view, lack Mind altogether; but otherwise everything is composed of everything. What, then, could define one thing as distinct from another? Aristotle's response [*Physics*,A4,187a23] to this question is most concise. He says that "the nature of each thing is thought to be determined by that of which it has a preponderance." To resume our focus on humanity, the implications of these beliefs and theories for human being are quite clear. Humanity, like everything else, in Thales' words is "full of gods." At the same time, humanity shares animal life with the beasts and is consequently "full of beasts." Yet, despite its share of bestiality and divinity, it is the consciousness of death, "mortality" in a word, which has preponderance in humanity, and so determines its nature.

In sum, ancient Greek humanism, which is the legacy received by Euripides, assigns to humanity a reasonable place within the full expanse of nature rather than unleashing human beings upon nature as unaccountable tyrants or plunderers. In contrast with this relatively benign and self-effacing humanism, Levi-Strauss, in a recent essay on "Race and Culture," [in *The View From Afar*, NY:Basic Books, 1985] says that en route to our more arrogant modern humanism "man had forgotten that he is worthy of respect more as a living being than as the lord and master of creation." Yet it is only fair to say that this is a forgetfulness which was already well on its way in Euripides' Athens and of which Euripides, drawing upon the more ancient tradition, was an unrelenting critic.

To bring this discussion home once more to the theatre of Euripides, I wish to claim that Euripidean drama, contrary to what Nietzsche would have us believe, is profoundly Dionysian. All that I mean by this claim will be made clear in time; but for our present purposes I wish to focus on his most explicitly Dionysian work, the *Bacchae*; for there we find Euripides' most devastating assault on the arrogant humanism lamented by Levi-Strauss as well as his most radiant articulation of the ancient truths that humanity is full of gods and full of beasts and thus required to find and to inhabit humbly that middle place assigned to it.

Before we can approach the *Bacchae* with any perception, we must dismiss a frequent and fundamental misconception of Dionysiac religion, namely that Dionysus is the god of the drunken debauch. Plutarch is nearer the truth when he says that Dionysus is the god of *hygra phusis*, literally "fluid nature," which encompasses all of the rippling, pulsing, erupting, sluicing forces of life: blood, water, sap, semen, milk and, admittedly, wine. Dionysus represents and presides over the unrestrained potency of animal life, in which human beings may commune. To drink from the *hygra phusis*, as we learn from the messenger's report to Pentheus, may be to drink water struck from rock or to drink milk scratched up from the soil or to drink the blood of animals torn apart in the frenzied *sparagmos*, as well as to drink wine spurting up from the face of a rock at the tap of Dionysus' wand. In whatever form, the bacchant is drinking the god and becoming one with him. This is the meaning of *baccheuein*: not

60

so much to revel, but rather to merge with the god Dionysus, to be transformed by union with the boundless forces of life, which defy and overrun every metaphysical and conventional border.

Thus, in the *Bacchae*, Dionysus himself is transformed from god to man to beast and back again. He takes any shape he wishes; and, beyond the city walls where the animals and the mountains are wild with divinity, he draws his bacchants into corresponding metamorphoses. Even the rigid Pentheus, who stands guard personally over the boundaries which describe and maintain civic and domestic life as he knows it, even Pentheus is lured into becoming one with the god and thus suffering unforeseen transformations. First, Pentheus takes the form of a woman and then, when he is totally one with the god - a union symbolized, on the one hand, by his vision of the two suns and, on the other, by his elevation in the arms of the tree sacred to the god - he is dragged down as both god and beast to be the prey and the sacred feast of women ecstatically alive with all that is both savage and sacred. Pentheus, who would stand off from the god and not be touched, becomes the surrogate of the god and suffers in his stead. In the end, under the aegis of a smiling god, it is he who is mourned and not the god; and so he enters the destiny waiting for him in his name, "Pentheus," the "mourned one."

From even this brief glance at the *Bacchae*, we see how it is that Dionysus is the god not only of religious mania and ecstatic rites but also of the mask and of theatre. He is the god of transformations, whether they occur in the mountains or in the streets or in the theatre. This is a god whose power suffices to erase, for a time, the lines between illusion and reality and thus to allow safe, at least in the theatre, passage across boundaries whose stability and maintenance are ordinarily required for human sanity and order. Both the borders of the metaphysical order and those of the political order become permeable in his presence and in his possession. In more contemporary terms, we would add that in the theatre a fissure is opened into the unconscious, providing for the controlled release of the unconscious into the conscious. In theatre, which endeavors to do more than entertain, the control is occasionally precarious and there is released a shudder of the primal panic which engulfed both Pentheus as he hurtled from his dendritic haven and Agave when she recognized her trophy as the same head which once, similarly

6 1

bloodied, had burst from her womb and brought her a similarly triumphant joy.

The bond between Dionysus and drama is, indeed, quite ancient, preceding by centuries the institution of Athenian tragedy. Dionysus was not in the fifth century a recent immigrant to Greece, as once thought, but seems instead to have been familiar to Greeks long before the year 1000. The Great Dionysia at which the tragedies were eventually performed dates only from the sixth century, while far more ancient was the Old Dionysia or the Anthesteria, also in the spring and also dedicated to the cult of Dionysus. The sequence of the Anthesteria, a three-day festival, bears certain similarities to the sequence of the Christian Passover, from the Passion to the Resurrection: the themes of sin and attonement, a communal meal in which the wine drunk is at the same time the blood of the dismembered god, and finally the restoration of the god in the midst of his devotees. More significant for our present discussion, however, is the fact that masked mummery and the veneration of the god made ritually present in his own mask were integral to this archaic festival, which means that Dionysus was affiliated with masks and with dramatic ecstasy already many centuries before the institution of the dramatic festival at the City Dionysia. In the latter festival, of course, the place of Dionysus was manifestly central. The dramatic contests were preceded by the sacrifice of a goat to Dionysus and by a procession to the theatre precinct where an effigy of the god was installed. The plays were literally performed in the presence of and to the god, with the priests of his cult near at hand. During the dramatic festival, the actors themselves were regarded as sacred officers of the Dionysian cult, one with the god as were his bacchants on the hillside of Thebes.

Although many formal elements of Athenian tragedy may well be traceable to dithyrambic choruses and explained as reasonable developments therefrom, the hot core, as it were, of ancient tragedy lies in the cult of Dionysus, god of masks, ecstatic transformation, and sacrificial immolation. The very name of tragedy [*tragoidia*], whose meaning remains a matter of dispute, may perhaps be appropriately translated as "song sung at the sacrifice of a goat"; for we know that the theatrical contests followed upon the sacrifice of a goat to Dionysus. The prize and the sacrificial victim associated with the dithyrambic contests was, on the other hand, not a goat but a bull. Tragedy, in fact, drew upon a number of pre-existing elements which it had in common with Dionysian and sacrificial ritual, such as the use of masks, song and dance at the *thumele* or sacrificial site, lamentation, and the music of the *aulos* or twin-flute.

In focusing on the Dionysian and sacrificial core of tragedy, the metaphysically definitive situation of tragedy is revealed. In the tragic theatre, humanity stands face to face with death and with the divine. The inescapable outcome is the disclosure of the human. Nowhere in the corpus of Athenian tragedy is this fact more visible than in the *Bacchae*, as Pentheus, confronted by his god and by death, unwittingly provides a spectacle from which the awful truth bursts forth. Seated in the precinct of Dionysus, the theatrical spectator might well say of Pentheus "there but for the immunity of the theatre go I." But the immunity of the theatre is finally an illusion. Pentheus too imagined that he was being provided a harmless spectacle at a safe distance; but he forgot that the tree in which he sat perched was sacred to Dionysus. He was already in the grip of the god. The theatre of Dionysus was no less the place of the god; and the spectators no less in the power of the god, soon to become the spectacle, unless they were to heed the god and to confront their own mortality. The *Bacchae*, it seems evident, is Euripides' consummate statement on the theatre; and thus these words [794-795], spoken through the mask of Dionysus, were aimed at all who at that moment confronted the god:

> Instead of raging on like this,
> Thrashing futilely against a force
>   that will never weaken,
> If I were you,
>   a man face to face with god,
>   I'd offer him a sacrifice.

If we examine the extant tragedies of Euripides, we find that with very few exceptions sacrifice figures substantially in their thematic development and often defines their very structure as, for example, with the *Electra*, the *Iphigeneia in Tauris*, the *Bacchae*, and the *Iphigeneia in Aulis*. However unorthodox and innovative Euripides may have been in many aspects of his work, he recognized the centrality of sacrifice and rooted his work more profoundly than did any of his fellow playwrights in this most sacred and revealing of all rituals, thus giving his work an archaic resonance as well as a source deep within the Greek psyche from which to launch his most savage attacks on the atrocities of his times. Consequently, if we are to reach the core of Euripides' work, we must explore the meaning of sacrifice in ancient Greek piety and thought and reveal how it was that both sacrifice and theatre served to delineate the metaphysical structure of the cosmos and, more particularly, the place of humanity within that structure.

Sacrifice [*thusia*] was the cornerstone of Greek religion, the primary and central religious activity in the fifth-century *polis*. Nearly all personal and civic acts of any significance - festivals, wars, athletic contests, births, deaths, marriages, oracular consultations, treaties, contracts - were marked by sacrifices. The act of sacrifice constituted the definitive experience of the sacred and, for that matter, of the human; for sacrifice clarified and acknowledged the relative status of the human and of the divine in the scheme of things. Apart from the *sphagia*, blood sacrifices performed for their own sake in extreme situations, before battle and at burials, the fundamental structure of sacrifice was that of ritual slaughter followed by a meat feast. In order to understand this structure and its significance, we will discuss each of these essential elements in turn.

Sacrifice is first and most evidently an act of slaughter. Life is violated and with it the bond between humans and beasts; for in all but the darkest and most distorted sacrifices, the victim is an animal. In cutting the throats of animals, human beings cut themselves loose from their intuitive communion with animals in life. Human beings cause and experience death and yet survive. In sacrifice, human violence is diverted to animals and sanctioned as an exception. Killing is contained by ritual and made to serve both the solidarity of humans with gods and the solidarity of humans with each other. In the violation of animal life, human beings turn their backs on the beasts; and, in sending up the sweet smoke of sacrifice, human beings turn to the gods, seeking their favor and their fellowship. By offering up the fruit of sacrifice to powers above the human, human beings consecrate and thus justify the savagery with which they have severed themselves from the beasts.

The second essential element of sacrifice is the meat feast, which may, of course, have been the primitive origin of and pretext

64

for sacrifice. In the feast, the victim is cooked with divinely derived fire and becomes human nourishment. The death of animal life serves to sustain human life. The encounter with death is followed by the shock of human survival and consequently the affirmation of human life in a feast. Complicity in the irrevocable act of killing, the shared experience of death, the terror it evokes and the guilt it instills, all conspire to create human solidarity. The focusing of human violence on animals, it is hoped, will divert that violence from fellow humans. Homicide and homophagy are to be renounced just as the killing and eating of animals are sanctioned. The survival of the human community is thus affirmed and assured by sacrifice; for when animals become the helpless victims of human violence, the source of human nourishment, and the acceptable outlet for human aggression, then the most primal threats to human survival are removed, namely hunger and the attacks of other animate beings, bestial or human.

Even though sacrifice opens up and establishes limited communion and communication with the gods, the distinct portions assigned to each make clear the divide which separates them. Humans receive the edible, perishable portions, a meal required by their own precariously perishable existence. The gods' portion, by contrast, is consumed in flames together with spices. What they receive is the sweet smoke and scent which rise out of human sight to delight those unimaginably remote beings who have no needs or fears.

The role that sacrifice plays, then, both in Greek religion and in Greek theatre, is to trace the most essential boundaries in the cosmos and thus to illuminate those truths which, if ever obscured, would condemn the world to darkest chaos. In the theatre, these boundaries are not only drawn but also transgressed. We learn best from contrast; and so we are made to witness both the brightest and the darkest of deeds, both crystalline clarity and impenetrable confusion. Human victims are held down under sacrificial blades, human flesh serves as human feast, mothers murder their children and children their mothers, brother slaughters brother. Every truth is denied, every nature defiled, so that they might be rediscovered and reaffirmed as the foundation of human fellowship and thus of the city. Unless the metaphysical order remains inviolate, the moral order cannot hold. In short, when human beings forget that they are distinct from gods and beasts, they begin to act like them. With this in mind, we return to these distinct categories so that we might come to a more precise and full understanding of each as they appear in the theatre of Euripides.

GODS

The traditional Greek gods belong, together with humans and beasts, to the one cosmos. Admittedly, their elevated status within the cosmic order confers upon them certain exemptions from necessities peculiar to human or bestial beings; but, for all their immunities and privileges, the Greek gods remain integral to the same world to which humans and beasts belong. Beyond this initial disclaimer of transcendence, however, it becomes quite problematic to formulate any concise, univocal account of ancient Greek theology. No such theology ever existed among the ancient Greeks; and therefore no scholarly or creative effort on our part can call it forth from the bleached stones of their temples and altars. The ancient Greeks had no sacred texts or prophets or formal priesthood with authority to decree official doctrine or discipline. It is, in fact, finally a misnomer to speak of ancient Greek religion at all. If we are to use the word "religion" with reference to ancient Greece, we ought to speak of "religions"; for there were civic, household, cthonic, rural, local, and pan-Hellenic gods and cults, all crowded into ancient Greek piety, not to mention an array of mysteries and brotherhoods complementing or challenging the more traditional beliefs and rites. We begin, then, with this awareness of the staggering complexity of ancient Greek piety so as to place the following modest reflections in appropriate perspective.

The first Greek poets to propose orderly, systematic accounts of the divine and human realms and their mutual affairs were Hesiod and Homer; and it was their visions more than any others that shaped the images and ideas of the gods within the subsequent literary tradition. The gods and goddesses highlighted by Homer were, of course, the Olympians, whom Hesiod identifies as latecomers created by earlier cosmic powers, such as Chaos, Earth,

Ocean, Sky, and Eros. In Homeric poetry, the earlier gods and goddesses of cthonic religion either lapse from sight altogether or appear in clear subordination to the Olympians. The traditional local heroes, who like the Christian saints display a proximity to the divine as well as unusual powers corresponding to that proximity, are also reduced in stature by Homer, particularly in the *Iliad*. Homer's heroes are without exception mortal and thus unambiguously removed from the divine realm. In Homer's patriarchal Pan-Hellenic vision, the primacy of the Olympians, and among them the preeminence of Zeus, is not to be challenged from any corner. What we must note even as we pass over it here is the fact that Homer's and Hesiod's conceptions of a pantheon of anthropomorphic gods and goddesses assembled on a mountain in the North, were common to virtually all of the ancient Aegean and Near Eastern world, with the exception of Egypt and Israel.

The blessed gods of Homer live altogether privileged lives. Their most singular privilege is, as we have already seen, their immortality. It is their immortality, however, which may be seen as the source of all that is petty and callous and shallow in them. Without having to pay the ultimate price for life, their lives are left without poignancy or purpose. They resemble rotten children unable to mature beyond their blindly wilful assertions and quarrels. To be sure, the Olympians are capable of grandeur and graciousness and occasional loyalty; but they are ultimately unreliable and disappointing from a human perspective. In their world nothing is irrevocable. The gods' wounds, like their errors, heal even as their human counterparts moulder in their graves. And apart from the fact that they "exist always" [*aien eontes*], they "live easy lives" [*rheia zoiontes*]. Unlike mortals whose already abridged lives are further reduced by necessities too numerous to count, the Olympians know only luxuriance and ease. The moral result is predictable. Without mortal tension in their fibers, they are incapable of sounding a pure note. Their courage and sorrow, laughter and love and grief are all pathetically imitative of human emotion and virtue. Apart from their power, the Homeric gods trail behind miserable mortals. Indeed, it seems not to have offended Greek piety to question the wisdom or the goodness of the gods. It was their power alone that was not to be doubted.

67

The Homeric pantheon, however pervasive its influence on Greek piety and imagination, was not without its critics. To many Greeks, the anthropomorphic character of the Olympians was ludicrous and offensive, all the more so because of the less than exemplary humanity mimicked by them. In the sixth century, Xenophanes, who seems to have been a deeply religious man, ridiculed Homer's gods, saying that "if cattle and horses and lions possessed hands, or were able to sketch and do the things men do, horses would draw gods that looked like horses, and cattle would draw gods resembling cattle, giving them bodies like their own." [fr.15] While he confessed that "there is no man nor will there ever be one who knows the truth about the gods," [fr.34] Xenophanes spoke of "one god, supreme among gods and mortals, in no way resembling mortals, either in body or in thought." [fr.23] Others sought to demythologize the Olympians by seeing in them poetic hypostases of cosmic forces or projections of human passions and folly. Empedocles, for example, gave the names of gods to the four universal elements. According to Prodicus, however, human beings divinize those things which benefit them most. In short, theories of the gods abounded, virtually all of them sceptical, if not contemptuous, of Homeric fundamentalism.

It may be said that Euripides, in his ideas of the gods, stood in a direct line from Xenophanes to Plato, who dismissed Homer as a seditious liar, regarded the encouragement of superstition as the worst crime against religion, and yet saw in atheism the breeding ground of tyranny. It may further be said that Euripides considered and echoed in his dramas a myriad of opinions concerning the gods. The first step towards honesty, if not clarity, in these matters is the admission of complexity and unknowing. Legend has it that Protagoras first read his notorious treatise "Concerning the Gods" in the home of Euripides, the opening statement of which is well-known: "Concerning the gods, I am unable to discern whether they exist or not, or what they may be like in form. The path to such knowledge is too strewn with obstacles, the subject too obscure, and human life too brief." Euripides seems to have taken to heart this cautious admission of his friend, which may be why we hear in his plays so many conflicting voices concerning the gods and things divine. When taking aim at elusive, even invisible, quarry, a scattergun would seem a wiser and less arrogant choice of armament than an arrow.

It must be stated from the outset, then, that Euripides' personal religious beliefs remain a matter of conjecture. As we form our own conjectures, however, it is mistaken to employ useless univocal categories such as theism, agnosticism, atheism, and secularism in an attempt to designate either Euripides or Athens in the late fifth century. Both are too conflicted and too complex to be so easily categorized. It is instructive in this regard to reflect on the inability of any such category to designate the religious convictions of Americans in the 1980's, Americans who, we know, comprise a spectrum from snake-handlers to sceptics, from those who refuse the services of combustion engines to those who deny any essential distinction between human spirituality and artificial intelligence. In some locations one can listen in vain for sacred words from church pulpits, while elsewhere bible hymns stream from variety store loudspeakers. If we hold a mirror, so to speak, to the soul of America, do we see reflected in it a believer or an atheist? In unwarranted despair we might retort at once that America is made up of millions of individuals calling for as many individualized mirrors. The truth is, however, that America in the late twentieth century, like Athens in the late fifth century, has a character which may very tentatively and provisionally be described, though not in simplistically satisfying terms. In sum, it is misguided to expect from the fifth century and from its poets a straightforward homogeneity which we would know better than to expect from our own and equally misguided to dismiss the possibility of ever reading one's own or others' times with any insight at all.

While Burckhardt's dichotomy of rationalism for the few and magic for the many is only once removed from sheer reductionism, it may be used to suggest the conflicted character of fifth century Athenian piety, which was both able to produce trenchant criticism of the religious tradition and barely able to tolerate that criticism. We may recall how the Athenian debacle in Sicily was partly occasioned by the paralysis of Nicias and the Athenian army in the face of a lunar eclipse. Pious observances and fears often lose their hold when they become inconvenient, much less lethal; but not so in this case, which suggests that they lay well below the skin. We may recall, as well, that the fifth century was scattered with impiety trials, as a result of which Protagoras was banished and Socrates executed. Anaxagoras was saved from prosecution only by the intervention of his friend Pericles; and we don't know what saved Euripides from the charges brought against him. The free thought for which Athens was known in the fifth century was apparently not without its price to pay. Even as we assume that Euripides might have been emboldened by the company of Athenian "free-thinkers," it is equally reasonable to assume that he may have been chastened by the quite effectual local forces hostile to any challenge raised against traditional piety. We know, for instance, from Plutarch that the line in the *Melanippe* [fr.480] which reads "Zeus, whoever that might be..." caused such an uproar in the theatre that Euripides, for a second production, altered it to read: "Zeus, as truth itself has said..." If Euripides was willing to rewrite a line, once written, we may assume that he was not above checking an impulse or reformulating an idea before it reached either the page or the stage. Just as Aristotle is thought to have masked and muted his own religious ideas so as to avoid repeating the fate of Socrates, it is surely possible that Euripides exercised a similar caution, lest he repeat the fate of Protagoras.

If there was any sanctuary of tolerance in Athens, however, it was the theatre, which enjoyed an astounding measure of "academic freedom" long before the founding of the academy. This freedom seems all the more remarkable when we remember that the theatre, apart from being a place of art and education, was also a sacred place, the temenos of Dionysus, whose cult image presided over the orchestra. The site for which Euripides wrote was closer to a church than a Broadway theatre, which we must keep in mind when we listen to words like these from Euripides' *Bellerophon* [fr.286], spoken face to face with Dionysus and within earshot, so to speak, of Athena Parthenos:

> Who is it, anyway, that says the gods exist
>   in starry heaven?
> They don't. They don't exist at all.
> Anyone still willing to talk
>   in that old-fashioned way
>   is a moron.

How, we might ask, are we to hear these words? It might seem that these and similar lines are singularly well-suited to modern scorn, so familiar as to require no interpretation. The opposite, however, is nearer the truth; for it is most unlikely that a contemporary audience or reader of Euripides will hear these words as blasphemy, which I suspect is what they are. Scorn is easily achieved; and indifference requires no achievement at all. Blasphemy is a different matter altogether from these and other common forms of secular disbelief. First-rate blasphemy, as T.S. Eliot has suggested in *After Strange Gods* [NY:Harcourt, Brace, 1934], may indeed be one of the rarest achievements in literature, requiring, in his words, "both literary genius and profound faith." He proceeds to explain that "no one can possibly blaspheme in any sense except that in which a parrot may be said to curse, unless he profoundly believes in that which he profanes." Obviously, the belief from which blasphemy spews forth is not a child's faith, seamless and unsullied. Rather, it is conflicted to its very core, wounded and wandering in pain. It has already been suggested by more than one scholar that the whole matter of the gods was for Euripides a source of incurable suffering; and such suffering is indeed the matrix of blasphemy.

At the very least, I wish to suggest here that fifth-century Athens was indeed a place where blasphemy could well have been uttered and, once uttered, understood. Very few, if any, such places still exist. Neither literary genius nor profound faith, much less their convergence, are in great supply in contemporary theatre. Profanity on the other hand, like the common dandelion, is annoyingly prevalent and unimpressive. Without celebrating blasphemy, it is nonetheless easy to understand Eliot's reproach for our age, in which he thought blasphemy had become a sheer impossibility.

Not so the age of Euripides. Dionysus, when accused of overreaction, answers quite simply in his own defense: "I am a god. I was blasphemed by you." [*Bacchae*,1347] And Dionysus was not singled out for this treatment. Zeus alone is treated with almost unexceptional deference and respect by Euripides, perhaps because Euripides may have come to regard the name of Zeus as a pseudonym of sorts for the unknowable god beyond all gods. Regardless, the lesser Olympians fare less well. To mention one, Apollo surely comes in for his share of blasphemy. In the *Ion* we are made witnesses to what may be called the birth of blasphemy. Ion,

7 1

the sanctimonious temple boy, is church-perfect when he enters the sacred precinct. His faith is dewy fresh. But as the shabby misdemeanors of Apollo are unfolded before his scrupulous eyes, he erupts with scandalized rage. The evidence overwhelms him. The gods flagrantly violate their own laws and still presume to punish men for their comparatively minor infractions of the same laws. He decides to confront Apollo with his wrongs; but Apollo is not to be confronted. Apollo is neither god enough to avoid sin nor man enough to own up to his sins once committed. The final blasphemy in the *Ion* is contained in the utterly damning no-show of Apollo in the final scene. The wrong divinity rides in on the machine. This theophany is transparent to a quite pathetic reality, the reality of a god cringing within earshot of the moral outrage of mortals and coaxing his bolder sister to talk him out of his dilemma. In the end, it is Apollo who indicts himself.

Apollo, as the god of divination and prophecy, comes in for additional abuse on this second count. The frequency and the ferocity of the attacks on oracles and auguries in Euripidean drama tempts one to infer from these some thorn deep in the author's spleen; but such conjecture is secondary to the fact of the affront itself, spilled out on sacred ground in words like these from the *Iphigeneia in Tauris* [572-575]: "The one real human tragedy is when we set aside our common sense and put our faith in oracles, only to be ruined by them." This same sentiment is echoed and amplified in the *Helen* [744-748] by a servant of Menelaus, a veteran of Troy, who is sick and angry over the part played by prophecy in that war and the sufferings it inflicted:

> You know, now I see the art of prophecy
>   for what it is,
>   a vulgar occupation and a pack of lies.
> Nothing useful came
>   from all the altar fires we lit,
>   nor from the winged screechings overhead.
> It's daft to dote on birds,
>   as if they're man's last hope.

Admittedly, in most Euripidean critiques of prophecy and divination, aim is taken not directly at the gods but at their human

72

agents, the race of priests and prophets, whose words are assessed as useless at their best and disastrous at their worst. One is often left to wonder whether there are, in the playwright's own view, any gods at all behind the dreams and oracles and auguries through which they were supposed to reveal their wisdom and their will. In any event, the human traffickers in supernatural insight made safer and surer targets of doubt and indignation. We may recall that even Plato seems to have given limited credence and place to knowledge gained through mantic experience. Not to have done so, at least officially, would have been to take a quite radical and possibly dangerous position, a position which we might suspect but cannot prove Euripides privately held.

Myth, like prophecy, is regularly discredited in Euripidean drama, though usually with less venom. Just as native wit and common sense are proposed as superior alternatives to oracles and divination, so myths are often crossed by more plausible accounts, closer to the realities experienced by the spectators. A frequent strategy employed by Euripides is to lay down the myth central to his drama as though it were the warp on his loom, and then to weave across the myth, as weft, polychrome threads of doubt, common sense, rational critique, and contradictory experience. Nowhere is this strategy more evident than in the *Helen*, wherein the accepted myth that Helen went off with Paris to Troy is crossed by the dramatic fact that Helen never went to Troy at all, but flew off to Egypt instead, in the arms of Hermes. The two stories and the two whereabouts of Helen are explained by there being two Helens, a phantom-Helen and the real Helen. Without our unravelling here the intricacies of this most vibrant and delightful Euripidean comedy, we may note that the drama predictably calls upon its characters to sort out the discrepancies in the stories they have been living and suffering for nearly twenty years and to accept the painful truths consequent upon those discrepancies.

I have spoken of the *Helen* as a comedy, because by any modern measure that is patently what it is. Granted, it was written for the tragic stage and in the tragic form; but it is light in its touch, happy in its outcome, and frequently comic, even broadly so. The *Helen* is, nevertheless, at the same time tragedy, which is to say that it contains an essential contradiction, a contradiction revealed not altogether wittingly by the loyal, life-long servant of Menelaus as he is sorting out

73

the two Helens and their stories and coming to the singular, startling truth, that Helen never went to Troy, that she was never once unfaithful and had pined like a perfect Penelope for her far-flung husband, in whose arms she is finally wrapped. Now, staring at the rapture of Helen and Menelaus' reunion, this shipwrecked and otherwise wrecked veteran of Troy makes a quite understandable remark and, in doing so, reveals a dark chasm beneath the bright cloud on which Helen and Menelaus are perched [700-707]:

SERVANT
Menelaus, help me to share your happiness.
I can see for myself **that** you're happy,
    yet I can't for the life of me figure out **why**.

MENELAUS
But old friend,
    this is **your** story as well as ours.

SERVANT
This woman...wasn't she the one..who..I mean...
    didn't she mete out our misery in Troy?

MENELAUS
No, not she. The gods made fools of us.
All we ever had of her was a pathetic effigy,
    modeled out of thin air.

SERVANT
Wait...let me get this straight.
What do you mean?
That we went through all of that...
    for nothing more than a puff of air?

In this brief exchange, the heart-sickening tragedy of war is laid bare, a tragedy from which Helen and Menelaus are insulated by their noble standing and their fairy-tale lives. Menelaus tries to convince the servant that the royal myth is one in which even he has a share; but the servant, unless he is a fool, knows that Helen and Menelaus' story-line splits from his own, the one into comedy and the

74

other into tragedy. Even if this truth is lost upon the servant, it is less likely to be lost upon the drama's spectators. A similar divide is visually evident in the *Bacchae* wherein Dionysus wears a comic, or at least a smiling, mask and Pentheus wears a tragic mask. The *Bacchae*, like the *Helen*, brilliantly confuses tragedy and comedy and in doing so discloses the cosmic divide between gods and mortals. Human tragedy is seen to constitute divine comedy. They are the warp and the weft, not only of Euripidean tragedy, but of the universe as well.

On a lesser scale, in myriad brief episodes and exchanges, myth is affronted and challenged in Euripidean drama. Again in the *Helen*, as Helen introduces herself to the audience, she relates the popular myth of her conception, according to which Zeus feathered himself as a swan and had his way with Leda. But Helen immediately follows her recounting of the myth with a dismissing quip: "if there's any truth to what they say," [21] she adds. Later, when a lost Greek named Teucer washes ashore in Egypt and provides Helen with news highlights from home the following exchange ensues [137-144]:

HELEN
What of Tyndareus' twin sons?
Are they dead or alive?

TEUCER
You hear both.

HELEN
Well, which do you hear more?
God! I have suffered so much already!

TEUCER
One story is that they've become gods,
made into stars to circuit the night sky.

HELEN
That story makes me glad.
But you say there is another version...

75

TEUCER
There is... that they slit their own throats
and bled out their lives...
victims to their sister's shame.
No more stories. I've wept enough already.

Once myth has become just another story, one version
among many, its authority is broken irreparably. It must stand or fall
now in the same terms as any other account of reality. Myth is still free
to inhabit and roam the Euripidean theatre. Euripides undertakes no
sweeping dismissal of myth, any more than does Plato. Instead, he
merely reduces myth to human scale and permits his characters to
form their own judgements in its regard, which they readily do.
When, for instance, in the *Trojan Women*, Helen argues for her life
that the entire Trojan mess was Aphrodite's doing, Hecuba doesn't
believe a word of it and adds that neither would anyone else with any
intelligence. The truth is, according to Hecuba, that Helen took one
look at Paris and her wits went the way of Aphrodite. After all,
explains Hecuba, Aphrodite is just another word for lust. Heracles is
equally incredulous of the myths of divine misbehavior, when, in the
Heracles, he confesses that he doesn't believe any of them, never
did and never will.

Heracles' disbelief in the myths of divine adultery and
tyranny, however, must not be confused with disbelief in the gods.
Like Hecuba, Heracles is concerned to preserve the honor of the
gods from all-too-human slander. "If god is truly god," protests
Heracles, "he is flawless, lacking nothing. [All those myths to the
contrary] are the malicious lies of poets." [*Heracles*,1345-1346]
Iphigeneia, conscripted to the bloody service of Artemis after her
miraculous rescue from the blade of Calchas, comes to a similar
defense of divine flawlessness in the *Iphigeneia in Tauris*. Against all
appearances and against all that has been handed down regarding
the goddess whom she serves, Iphigeneia raises her own solitary
protest [381-391]:

> We mortals are unclean,
> forbidden to approach the goddess,
> if we soil our hands with bloodshed, touch a
> corpse,

76

or assist a woman giving birth.
And yet she herself revels in human sacrifice,
    finds it sweet.
No, this cannot be.
Zeus, and Leto his bride,
    cannot have spawned anything so spurious.
I don't believe the tales of Tantalus
    and his feast.
I don't believe that gods ever savored
    the flesh of a child.
Here in this land,
    men not gods are murderers.
Men make their own perversions into rituals
    and sacralize their sins.
No god is evil -
    that is what I believe.

Whether Euripides believed the same, we can never know. What we do know, however, is that this conviction - "if gods do anything shameful, they are not gods" [fr.292.7] - is expressed with frequency and passion in Euripidean drama, which allows us to say that there is in that drama an heuristic movement beyond the capricious and corrupt gods of the poets towards a more pure conception of divinity, less likely to offend human intelligence and integrity. Into the theological vacuum left by the poets and their myths, Euripides introduced a range of speculations current in his day. In fact, Euripides is commonly reckoned a disciple of Anaxagoras, whom Aristotle regarded as the first sober metaphysical thinker. Anaxagoras gave the name of Mind [Nous] to his First Cause, which brought order into the primordial chaos and then withdrew. It was Mind that initiated the rotary motion which drove the hot, dry, light, and rare seeds to the furthest edges of the universe to form aither. These speculations are of interest here because of the frequent occurence of Mind and of Aither as divine epithets in Euripidean drama, both the fully extant dramas and the fragments of lost dramas. "In each one of us it is the Mind that is God" [fr.1018] reads one fragment, while another refers to Aither, "which is known to mortals by the name of Zeus." [fr.877] In addition to Mind and Aither, other natural elements and forces, such as Earth and

Necessity, are given the name of God or Zeus in one or other Euripidean text.   There seems to be little point, however, in marshalling a fuller array of such references here; for from them we are able to conclude no more than that Euripides must have been keenly aware of and interested in the most advanced metaphysical thinking of his day.

In the midst, perhaps we may say the muddle, of theological speculation in Euripidean drama, most critics eventually indicate where they imagine Euripides' personal convictions to have been located. It may be justified, though not kind, to say of this endeavor to disclose the true mind of Euripides what was said of the notorious "search for the historical Jesus," namely that each critic, staring down into the well of history to catch a glimpse of Jesus' (read Euripides') own countenance, eventually with an elated sense of discovery glimpses his or her own face. Having said this, I foolishly take my place at the rim of the same well.

The dazzling scope of theological opinion in Euripidean drama suggests to me that Euripides neither possessed nor sought to promulgate any doctrine of the divine, even though the question of god remained a central and agonizing one for him. As we shall explore more fully in its proper time, the most urgent focus of Euripidean concern is the human realm, in particular the suffering which mortals endure from inhuman sources as well as the suffering which mortals endure from each others' stupidity and malice. The truth of God has direct bearing, however, on both sources of suffering, inhuman and human; for justice, whether cosmic or political, is man's only hope for respite. And justice, divine or human, is a religious matter for Euripides. "Justice has great power," says the chorus of the *Electra* [958]; and, for Euripides as for Homer, whatever has great power is somehow divine. Thus, in searching for the voice of Euripides among all the myriad voices resonant in his dramas, I imagine myself to hear something of his voice in these lines from the *Hippolytus* [189-197]:

> Human life, from beginning to end,
>   is riddled with pain.
> There is no respite from its burdens.
> But something other,
>   more deserving of love than life itself,

lies wrapt in darkness,
veiled in cloudy vapors.
We are revealed as we are,
hapless lovers of a brilliance
gleaming beyond our earthly reach.
No one can lay it bare for us.
Beyond this one mortal life,
we are inexperienced,
drifting aimlessly,
carried along by myths.

Indeed, "there is in the human circle no clear and bright truth about divine things." [*Heracles*,62] Human confusion and unknowing do not, however, preclude human longing and hope, which are precariously proposed in these choral lines from the *Hippolytus* [1103-1107]:

The care of the gods for me,
Whenever my heart welcomes such a thought,
Is a great thing.
It draws from me the poison of my pain.
But the secret hope I cherish,
That some kind Wisdom prevails,
Slips away from me,
When I watch what mortals do
And what they endure.

The care of the gods for mortals is left in considerable doubt in Euripidean drama. The hearts of the gods are called "inflexible" [1268] in the *Hippolytus*, while Artemis says of herself and her Olympian colleagues that it is their custom to remain always "aloof and neutral" [1130]. Artemis, forbidden by heavenly law to weep and to look upon the dead, abandons her devotee in his moment of most profound need and wins his ironic rebuke: "it's a slight matter for you to turn your back on a long companionship." [1441] The gods, Olympian or otherwise, appear fickle. One moment they preside over human affairs, moulding them in their hands like soft clay; the next moment they are gone, deaf to human appeal, blind to human agony. And so it is in the Euripidean theatre. In the *Bacchae*, the god is in

79

total control. There is no crack in which one might hide from his power. In the *Hecuba*, however, Hecuba can no more raise a god than she can breathe her children back to life.

The power of the gods, as has already been said, is not the decisive question in Euripidean drama, any more than it is in the *Book of Job*. It is the justice of the gods that concerns mortals most; for, if the gods are not just, their existence and their power are no consolation at all. And, despite the occasional assertion of divine justice in the Euripidean theatre, justice remains therein predominantly a human concern and a human challenge. The following fragment [506] from the lost *Melanippe* may indeed express something of the mind of Euripides on this matter:

> Do you really think that injustices
>   sprout wings and fly before the gods,
>   where Zeus has them inscribed on tablets,
>   for his own records,
>   so that he can study them,
>   and administer justice to mortals below?
> The firmament itself would not suffice
>   to contain Zeus' records of human sins.
> Nor would Zeus himself be equal to the task
>   of sorting out the sins of humankind
>   and meting out to each his due.
> No, justice is already here,
>   close by us,
>   something you will see,
>   if you care to open your eyes to it.

It may well be that "human virtue accomplishes nothing without the efficacious favor of the gods." [*Suppliant Women*,596-597] Even so, most Euripidean characters seem convinced that without human virtue, most specifically without human justice, the efficacious favor of the gods will likewise accomplish next to nothing. The gods cannot reap what they do not sow. "There is as much chaos among the gods," suggests Iphigeneia, "as there is among humans." [*Iphigeneia in Tauris*,572-573] Finally, however, the fact that the gods have their own hands full or that they are themselves unjust or that they interfere in human affairs only at whim from a general position of indifference, all of these and other common Euripidean criticisms are contained in the undeniable metaphysical fact that the gods are inhuman. It is their inhumanity that says everything. The sheer distance of the gods accounts for all of their human shortcomings and renders inestimable and unreliable their virtues.

The ground of all human fellowship is equality, communion in a shared humanity; and the gods are simply excluded from this fellowship. Aristotle recognized this in the *Ethics* when he said that friendship or love [*philia*] cannot exist between two beings when a gulf of inequality divides them. The example he gave was the gulf between god and humankind, which precludes fellowship between them. "No one needs friends," says Theseus in the *Heracles* [1338], "when he is cherished by the gods." Theseus spoke these words, however, even as he held out his hand in friendship to the broken, all-too-human Heracles. There is no confidence whatsoever in Euripidean drama that human beings are cherished by the gods, which would argue that Euripidean "theology" points, at the end of the day, to humanity and to human fellowship. In this case, we are left with the last words of Heracles [1425-1426], once a would-be god who has in the meantime left behind every illusion of divinity and suffered his way to the human border only to drink the unexpected sweetness of friendship: "any man who would prefer great wealth or power to love, the love of friends, is sick to the core of his soul."

HUMANS

Second in status within the metaphysical order, suspended somewhere between the gods and the beasts, humans take up a peculiarly precarious existence. As has been pointed out already, the human condition is fraught with ambiguity, drawn as it is from two disparate, immiscible sources: the divine sphere of continuous being and the bestial sphere of continuous becoming. The radical instability of human being as imagined by the ancient Greeks may be grasped as soon as we realize that in Greek myth human being is not privileged with a clear and distinct creation. Unlike Hebrew and other

81

Near Eastern mythologies, Greek mythology contains no account of a divine creation of human being. The Greek gods are quite capable of extinguishing human life but not of originating it. Like human beings, the Greek gods may participate in the natural process of human procreation, provided they seduce or seize a human partner; but the gods stand no nearer to the origin of that process than do their human consorts. Human being, as the ancient Greeks strove to understand it, came to be seen as the realization of a process of separation from divinity, on the one hand, and from bestiality, on the other. Humanity, in short, came to be understood as the product of a temporal process, an "original" process which must nevertheless be reflected and reaffirmed in the life of each individual human being.

Broadly speaking, there were already at the time of Euripides two quite irreconcilable anthropological theories offering divergent accounts of humanity's beginnings and of the human process into the present. The one imagined human being to have come to its current condition through a process of decline from an original state of near-divinity, while the other imagined human being to have arisen slowly from an original state of near-bestiality. In neither view had human being been uniquely fashioned, breathed into life, and assigned its proper place and purpose in the order of the cosmos. Rather, it was agreed from either side that human being had arrived at its current middle position within the metaphysical order from somewhere else. Whether that "somewhere else" was nearer to the state of the gods or nearer to that of the beasts was a matter sharply disputed. Either human being was descended from some sublime, superior being or human being was evolved from some brutish, savage being. Finally, each of these theories presented a distinct moral imperative to human being, understood to be ever-mutable and ever in process. If human being had regressed from an originally idyllic condition, it remained for it to retrace its steps, however it might, back to that first, most perfect state. If, however, everything in the human past represented darker, denser, more barbarous conditions, it fell to human being to hold the ground it had gained and to take further steps, if possible, into civilization.

Foremost among the proponents of the first theory - that humanity had regressed to its current condition - were Hesiod and Plato; and now, in order to explore this theory in somewhat fuller detail, we turn to Hesiod, whose views were surely altogether familiar to Euripides. According to Hesiod, there was once, under the reign of Cronus, a golden age of men - I say "men" advisedly, since woman had not yet been fashioned into existence - in which gods and men, though distinct beings, lived in close proximity and fellowship. They shared the same feasts, for which neither of them toiled; for life in the golden age was free of pain, relieved of the necessity for labor. There were no wars, no contention, no killing, and no sexual union. Men were uniformly of high moral character; yet, for all their near perfections, they were mortal. Death, even then, had its claim on humanity; but it came gently, like sleep. Of course, neither we nor Euripides require the informative services of Hesiod to notice that human prerogatives have undergone severe slippage in the intervening ages of man. As for the consummate curse upon man in the Hesiodic account, the creation of woman and the gods' inflicting of her upon man, we will soon consider that event in its proper place within the political order.

The second theory - that humanity had progressed to its current condition - may be found in the Homeric Hymn to Hephaestus and was proposed by a range of later writers such as Protagoras, Critias, Moschion, and Diodorus. Of more direct interest here is the fact that it is quite frequently invoked or alluded to in the dramas of Euripides. The many varied versions of this theory are complex beyond the scope of any exploration we might conduct here; but even a distilled, composite account will suit our present needs. The foundational idea here is that humanity once lived in a beastly condition, dwelling in caves and engaging in frightfully uncivilized practices, including cannibalism. A number of pre-Socratic thinkers took one further retrogressive step in the argument and claimed that humanity began its long career quite literally as an animal, quite possibly some other animal altogether. Anaximander conjectured, in this regard, that the first humans were produced within fishes and nourished until they were competent to make their own way on land, at which point they were cast up on the shore. Archelaus, on the other hand, argued that human beings had emerged originally as a hybrid, resulting from interbreeding among animals.

In the midst of these early anthropological speculations on humanity's bestially humble beginnings, various proposals were set forth to explain how and by what humanity was decisively distinguished from animals. Some pointed to fire and to the

83

transforming arts which it made possible, while others suggested that specifically human life emerged with the cultivation of grain and the domestication of animals. The polis too, with its own distinct order, the political order, articulated in its laws, seemed to some to mark the decisive emergence of human civilization. Speech, thought, intelligence, and moral sensibility were also candidates for humankind's specific difference from the other animals. Even the gods were, on occasion, given credit for raising humankind from its primal destitution to its moderately privileged status above its former peers. "I praise that god," says Theseus in the *Suppliants* [201-204], "who lifted humanity from its primal confusion and parted humanity's path from that of beasts, first with the gift of intelligence and then with that of language..."

In fact, all of the above proposals find expression in one or other Euripidean drama, from which fact we may conclude at the very least that Euripides took an active interest in current anthropological speculations, just as he did in theological ones. Needless to say, such ranging speculations on humanity's origins and progress provided Euripides with a wealth of images and ideas which he could turn to his own dramatic purpose and profit. In the *Cyclops*, for example, Euripides was able to employ nearly the full array of such ideas to contrast the purportedly advanced political civilization of Odysseus, who was clearly standing-in for more contemporary swashbuckling Greeks, with the primitive, near-bestial community composed of the cannibalistic Cyclops and his shepherding satyr-serfs. The tongue and wits of Odysseus prove corrupt and ineffectual; and his only contribution to the island is to promote drunkenness and provoke violence. Reduced to primal desperation by the savage slaughter and consumption of his men, Odysseus re-invents the earliest primitive weapon effective at some distance, the Palaeolithic spear hardened by fire. Quite likely, beyond having a bit of fun, Euripides was in the *Cyclops* employing his characteristic irony to question just how far humanity, in the carriage of civilization, particularly Greek civilization, had truly progressed.

To return now to the core of our argument, we must note that the underlying assumption of both ancient accounts of humanity's essential process, whether understood as regress or progress, is that human being is unstable and ambiguous, requiring definition for the sake of clarity and resolve for the sake of integrity. Thus human being is seen as the fruit of human becoming, which is both a pre-historical and a personal phenomenon. Ancient anthropology addresses the "becoming" of humankind, while ancient ethics addresses the "becoming" of the human individual. What distinquishes ancient anthropological considerations, then, from ethical ones is a matter of respective scale rather than of substance. Finally, it must be stated that the scale of ancient drama coincides far more closely with that of ethics than with that of anthropology; for drama thinks and speaks and moves through stories, the stories of individual lives, however transparent those lives may be to the myriad spectrum of humanity. The appropriate span of time recommended by Aristotle for each tragic drama was the circuit of one day's sun across the sky, which no plays seem to have exceeded to the extent required to trace the path of humanity from the golden age or from the bellies of fish to its present condition.

Euripidean drama, however scattered it may be with references or allusions to anthropological speculations or, for that matter, to theological speculations, finds its center in the ethical problem of human becoming. In order to press now to the heart of this problem, it is instructive to recall from the preceding discussion of the gods that it was their inhumanity which in the end proved definitive of their nature and decisive for all of their qualities; and the root of their inhumanity lay in their immortality. The final insignificance of the Greek gods and the ultimate frivolity of divine affairs may be traced to their conscious inexperience of death. Correspondingly, human significance and the consummate seriousness of human affairs may be traced in Euripidean drama to the conscious experience of death, which is what is meant by mortality.

With a few fanciful exceptions which serve only to prove the rule, all human beings potrayed or considered in Greek poetry are mortal [thnetoi], just as all gods are immortal [athanatoi]. To say this is, however, to say a good deal more than simply that all human beings die and that all gods do not. If this were the case, goats and bulls and birds would be mortals; for surely their eventual demise is as certain as ours. But they are not mortals, despite their being yoked to death. What they lack is not death but the consciousness of death. They live and then they die, while mortals live and die at once. Beasts live as if they will live forever, even though they will not; for they do not know in their minds and hearts that from the first moment of their lives

85

they face death. It is the conscious anticipation of death and the transforming power which such anticipation exercises over a life that comprise mortality. The fact of death alone is without significance, like a geometric point without extension. As we have seen already and will see again, the fact of death is critical; for otherwise gods with all their consciousness could manage to be mortal, which they can never be. The mere fact of death, then, is critical but insufficient for mortality.

To be mortal [*thnetos*] is to be "deathful"; and life is only full of death when it is infused and heightened with the consciousness of death. Once again, we find humanity spread-eagled across the metaphysical spectrum, bound to share both the consciousness of the gods and the doom of dumb animals. To be born of woman, however, does not bestow mortality other than as a destiny and a debt. The same is to be said precisiely of human being; for human being and mortality are finally one. All that birth brings with it is human possibility, which must be realized personally in the process of human becoming, mortal becoming, which is at its core a coming to the consciousness of death and an embracing of the ethical consequences of that consciousness. We will consider first the coming to mortal consciousness and then its ethical consequences.

Whether we look to the Epic of *Gilgamesh* or to the *Iliad* or to the dramas of Euripides or to the dialogues of Plato, we find that mortal consciousness emerges through the power of human imagination, what Plato calls *eikasia*. *Eikasia*, as Plato understands it, is the human capacity to see an image as an image. An animal sees images straight on as visible objects. As Leonardo daVinci explains in his notebooks, a dog may well run to a painting of its master, as if the painting were the master; but as soon as the dog licks the painting, the painting becomes mere paint. One moment the painting is the master and the next moment it is not. It is either the one or the other. At no point is it, for the dog, an image of the master. The curious thing about an image is that it both is and is not what it is. A bust of Pericles, for example, **is** Pericles. At the same time, however, it **is not** Pericles; for Pericles is no more and never was this or any other bust. Nonetheless, we humans look at a carved bust of him and say that "this is Pericles", by which we mean that we see Pericles in it. It is this same capacity to see one reality reflected in another that is refined and exercised at each critical point of turning in the ascent of Plato's divided line in the *Republic*. In short, Platonic wisdom is rooted and realized in the power and practice of human imagination.

Imagination is no less essential to Euripidean theatre than it is to Platonic metaphysics; for *eikasia* is not always mystical in its aspirations. We reach at once the heart of tragic imagination when we realize that human beings can die without dying, can confront death without passing through its portals; for human beings can see their own deaths reflected in the deaths of others. Gilgamesh, when he holds and beholds the head of his dying friend Enkidu, his other self, dies with him and then returns to life. He returns to life, however, transformed; for he now sees death as well as life in all things, including himself. He is full of death, just as he is full of life. The metaphysical truism that in humanity the immiscible streams of being and nonbeing converge becomes a volatile, enlivening, obliterating truth for Gilgamesh as it does for Achilles in the *Iliad* and for Admetus in the *Alcestis*. Achilles, after lying with his lost friend through the long night, stripped naked of any illusion of immortality, rises and stands off from the corpse of his other self. The metaphysical dikes give way and the full ambiguity of his humanity descends on him. He is at once a blazing god and a ravaging animal. He is, briefly, the savage, celestial event of their release and collision.

In Plato's metaphysical scheme, imagination is revelatory precisely because the cosmos is constituted as an ascending series of images. One reality reflects another, which in turn reflects another, until our minds are drawn to that reality which reflects nothing but simply **is**. Correspondingly, within the ethical and literary spheres, imagination is revelatory because all of history is constituted as a series of human lives, in each one of which we can see ourselves somehow reflected. Each life is an image of humanity, a moving, fleeting, imperfect image with which we have a deep affinity created by the fact that we too are, each of us, images, woven of being and nonbeing, fraught with life and with death. Finally, when we consider that the Greek theatre is peopled with masks and that those masks are images reflecting both the personages of myth and the citizens of Athens, then the theatre too becomes revelatory, a place of essential disclosure. In sum, the structure of the Euripidean theatre, like that of the Platonic cosmos, is comprised of icons or images and requires imagination at every turn to see images as images, masks as masks,

87

and so in them and through them to reach insight. Platonic *peripeteia*, enacted in the ascent from sensory images to divine Being is at final odds, however, with Euripidean *peripeteia*. The end of Platonic wisdom is to think divine thoughts, whereas the end of Euripidean wisdom is to think human thoughts.

So that these seemingly incidental reflections on imagination might be brought now to a sharp and suitable focus, we turn to the earliest of Euripides' extant dramas, the *Alcestis*, in which the *peripeteia* or critical turning of Admetus to the truth of his humanity occurs through what we have described as poetic *eikasia*, or imaginative insight. What we must realize from the outset about Admetus is that the extraordinary luxuriance and privilege of his condition have made of him an *idiotes*, a man radically inexperienced in the common limits of humanity. He lives in a world of his own, a world so unique as to reflect nothing beyond itself. In addition to having inherited the ease and privileges of royalty, Admetus has the god Apollo for his slave, the hero Heracles for his friend, and has for his wife a woman willing to take his place in death. How is such a man to think human thoughts?

The first blow to Admetus' illusory insulation from the human condition is struck strangely enough by his wife Alcestis. After she whispers her last goodbye and leaves his arms holding her cooling corpse, Admetus' first words are: "In my misery I am slain" or "I am lost in misery" (*apolomen talas*,391). The word which he uses here to describe the effect which Alcestis' death has on him means to be killed or slain or annihilated or lost. Of course he is literally none of these. Instead, he is presumably in flawless health, with a new lease on life. His words literally describe not himself but Alcestis. The truth is, nonetheless, that Admetus has endured something quite unexpected. He has, in part, died with Alcestis. His immunization from humanity has proved imperfect and let him down. He is undermined by his own inalienable human imagination; for he has seen and experienced his own death in Alcestis' death. He is not as yet fully aware, however, that this is what has happened to him. Still less has he followed that awareness to its full mortal and ethical conclusions. For the moment, he displays the stunned disorientation and depression of an animal mourning the death of its mate in uncomprehending confusion. He is coming to human

88

consciousness, slowly and painfully. He is coming to it from a great distance.

For the lesser members of his household, whose education into the human consortium had begun at birth, the truth of Admetus' situation is obvious. He has not been singled out to endure some unique swat of fate; rather, he has reenacted a commonplace. In the words of the chorus of common citizens, which is to say in the words of common sense [416-419]:

> Admetus, your misfortune is not optional.
> You must endure it.
> After all, you are not the first man alive,
> Nor the last,
> To lose a good wife.
> Try to understand.
> Dying is something expected of us all.

For a time, Admetus keeps his rage. He clings to the conviction that he has been singularly wronged. But by whom? For lack of a more suitable or proximate culprit, Admetus unleashes his outrage on his father, Pheres, who has refused to die in Admetus' stead and so, in Admetus' distorted vision, deserves to be cursed as the most selfish of men. Pheres, however, is not prepared to accept the blind, insulting fury of Admetus and spits Admetus' words back at him with shocking savagery. This, in abridged form, is what he has to say to his son [675ff]:

> Listen, boy,
> > just who do you think you're cursing out?
> I gave you life,
> > made a man of you,
> > left you with mastery over my house.
> I'm not obliged to die for you.
> When my turn to die comes, leave it to me.
> I'll do the same for you.
> The fact is, to squeeze free of death,
> > you waged a shameless campaign.
> Well, your time came and went;
> > and you've still got your life.

All you had to do was murder your own wife.
You've obviously stumbled on a brilliant scheme
    for private immortality.
It's only a matter of convincing
    your "wife of the hour"
To do your dying for you.
Take this much from me:
    the rest of us are as fond of our lives
    as you are of yours.

      The fact is that Admetus finds himself less fond of his life now without Alcestis. He begins to live the life emptied of life and to nurse the never-healing wound predicted for him by the chorus and Alcestis' maid. He returns to an empty house and an empty life with a palate so embittered that the future can promise him no sweetness. Neither the radiant sun overhead nor the soft, rich soil beneath his feet have the slightest consolation to offer him in his pain. He envies the dead, particularly his wife. Relentlessly, the chorus interrupts his tiresome, self-indulgent laments and reminds him that all of this is nothing new and that, if his pain seems so without precedent, it is only because he was so inexperinced when grief struck.
      The final episode of *Alcestis*, when the broken, humbled, and struggling Admetus encounters Heracles and his prize, the mysterious veiled woman so like Alcestis, is too complex and elusive to admit of easy distillation here. Nonetheless, I will venture several tentative comments. Whatever a lifting of the woman's veil might reveal is less critical than what Admetus reveals in this encounter; for, apart from poetic license, there is no return from death. Even if this Greek fairy tale is given a happy ending, life is not so blessed. Admetus has learned this much and struggles briefly with its implications. He is still a child, unequal to the demands of mature integrity. What he has outgrown is not his weakness but his blindness. He is transparent even to himself in his failures, his failed friendship to Heracles and his failed vows to the dying Alcestis. Her honor, he admits, has its claim on him; but both his weakness and the fantastic premise of this play preclude his respecting that claim. After all, this was not a tragedy but a satyr-drama, despite the absence of satyrs. It is, in the words of an ancient commentator, tragedy at play. Its playful premise, however, is, like the prize of Heracles, thinly

veiled. Anyone who knows that death's word is final can lift the veil or simply peer through it, and then go on to complete the tragedy of Admetus.

What Admetus only begins to glimpse before his tragedy is ludicrously interrupted are the claims that mortal consciousness place upon him. Pheres inflicted upon him the awareness that others cherish their lives as deeply as he does his. Presumably, then, Alcestis loved her life as deeply as Admetus loves his. The damning brilliance of this truth reaches even the depths of Admetus' encaved self-absorption and reveals him for what he is, a moral troglodyte until now snugly sheltered from the human realm. For Admetus to learn the truth that human life is each time precious and each time doomed required that Alcestis die and that Admetus go down into imaginative death with her. It is not a truth one learns on one's own. Human beings teach it to each other by living and dying and suffering. Sooner or later, in the face of the human spectacle, imagination eats away the self's protective secretions and the illusion of uniqueness is lost. We see our own death in the deaths of others. We come to despise the safe distance which we, like the ancient gods, would have kept from self-polluting communion in wretched humanity. We may recall how Theseus reprimanded his mother, Aethra, when she made her own the sufferings of the Argive women who had lost their sons in the seige of Thebes. "Their troubles are no reason for you to groan," Theseus instructs Aethra; for "you are not one of them." [*Suppliant Women*,291,292] What he says literally is that she is not born or descendent [*ephus*] from them, that she does not have the same nature [*phusis*]. Kinship, for Theseus, is a matter of blood. He sees and feels the sufferings of his family, and perhaps of his city, as his own; but his imagination is not yet so lucid and embracing as to see the sufferings of any human being as his own. I say "not yet" because we learn of Theseus, after he has been instructed in the ills of humanity, that he himself has gone down into the carnage and is washing the filth of battle from the corpses of the fallen warriors. We may presume that the herald speaks for Theseus when, in response to a shocked comment on how unspeakably shameful such work is, he answers: "What shame can there be in bearing our common human ills?" [768] Clearly, Theseus has come to see for himself what his mother saw from the beginning.

The first profound implication of mortality is fellowship, the fellowship of the doomed. Nowhere in Greek literature is this truth more strangely invoked than in the fatal encounter between Achilles and the young Lycaon, who must be counted one of the unluckiest of Priam's or anyone else's sons. Armed only with his pleading, Lycaon grips Achilles' spear with one hand and his knee with the other hand; but no number of gestures or words will save him, because Achilles is daimonically deathful on this day. He has indeed caught the chill of death from sleeping with the corpse of Patroclus through the dark, silent night. What is at first hearing so strange, however, is the mannner in which Achilles welcomes Lycaon into the fellowship of the doomed with the greeting "friend" [*Iliad*,XXI.106-110]:

Friend, you too must die.
Why spend your tears and your cries
On me? Patroclus, you know, is dead;
And you will never be the man he was.
Are your eyes blind to me?
To my beauty, my stature, the fact
That my father is a splendid man
And my mother a daughter of heaven?
Yet death stalks me as much as you.
Nor am I an equal to my fate.

When he heard this, we are told that both Lycaon's spirit and his knees failed him; for he knew himself in that moment to be a dead man. Compelled to gaze imaginatively both upon the already dead Patroclus and upon the soon to be dead Achilles, Lycaon was emptied of hope. The *Iliad* is replete with such leaps of imagination and the unlikely fellowship which they create. Surely the greatest imaginative leap of all is when Priam and Achilles, their eyes washed pure with tears, gaze across the abyss which divides them and wonder at the sight before them. Achilles sees in the aged, mournful Priam his own old and miserable father, while Priam sees in the wondrous Achilles his own once-resplendent son. Achilles too thinks of Hector and weeps for Patroclus. The two of them draw together in their thoughts, embrace in their grief, break down, and fill the tent with their cries. Their tears and their laments mingle; for

92

theirs is a single, immeasurable sorrow. Later, Achilles rises, takes Priam's arm, and gently lifts him to his feet. "Without a care of their own, the gods weave for us mortals lives of sorrow," he says to Priam. "For us to live is to grieve." [XXIV.525-526]

The fellowship to which Achilles invites Priam is very close to that which he extended to Lycaon, except that murderous passion has given way in the meantime to mournful compassion. Achilles stood over the helpless Lycaon both as a ravaging beast and as a glaring god. He meets Priam, however, face to face, as a human being who endures with him the caprice of the gods. This, I believe, is the consummate moment of vision in the *Iliad*, the moment of truth, in which a new model of human community emerges. The human order revealed herein rests neither upon the spear nor upon the sceptre, neither upon brute force nor upon divine prerogatives. The true human order rests, it seems, upon mortal compassion; and the appropriate scope of *philia*, the bond of human love, is not familial, not civic, nor ethnic, but universal; for there are few divides between mortals, either in literature or in life, greater than that between Priam and Achilles.

This, then, is the meaning of imaginative insight: to see one reality in another, or to see one reality and to think another. What occurs in such moments is not confusion but crystalline clarity. When Achilles looks at Priam and imagines his father, and when Priam looks at Achilles and imagines his son, their vision is heightened not muddled. It is not as if properly separate realities are running together like pigments in the seething cauldron of their souls. The truth is, rather, that these two grief-chastened men are no longer sufficiently arrogant and wilful to fracture and disperse into separate realities what is essentially one. When pigments mix they turn to blackness; but when colors, bands of light, converge they are luminous and pure white. This metaphor brings us closer, I believe, to what Heraclitus meant by the one light of day, the light of the waking world which we inhabit in common, the light of reason, in which each human life becomes transparent to each other human life in the hopeless, compassionate fellowship of mortals. In this light the truth of human nature is disclosed. This same light, the light of the common human realm, is altogether luminous in Euripidean drama.

It may seem to require a similar imaginative leap to pass from Homer to Euripides, from archaic epic to classical theatre; but the truth is that, in the moments which we have been considering from the *Iliad*, we are already well within the mind of Euripides. In the *Iliad*, after all, we may trace the tragic *peripeteia* of Achilles from the folly of his quarrel with Agamemnon to the wisdom of his fellowship with Priam. He goes down into death with Patroclus and emerges deathful. He sees only death in all eyes and in all things. In time, however, this passion gives way to compassion and he embraces, in *philia*, in the loving fellowship of wretched mortals, the father of his own greatest grief and of his final ruin. This movement of consciousness and the foundational human truths which it lays bare and brings to light pervade and shape Euripidean drama. In fact, it may be said that the radically new conception of human *arete* or excellence, the radically new definition of heroism, proposed by Euripides already shone centuries earlier in the tent of Achilles. It was not, however, what Euripides' contemporaries remembered best or honored most in the *Iliad*. What Euripides did was to rediscover that seed and plant it afresh in the fifth-century Athenian theatre. Here as elsewhere, it was Euripides' genius to discern the future in the past, to find something radically challenging in something ancient and forgotten.

The above claim that Homer, particularly in the *Iliad*, struck a well from which Euripides drank deeply must, of course, be tested against the full range of Euripidean drama; and such a test exceeds the modest limits of this book. Short of such a thorough test, however, it is to be hoped that this brief Homeric commentary finds frequent reflection and resonance in what has already been said and in what remains to be said herein about the voice and vision of Euripides, to which essential human fellowship, compassion, and love are so utterly central.

To conclude, now, this discussion of the human realm and of human becoming, we turn first to the *Heracles* and finally to the *Hippolytus*; for in both of these dramas the eponymous heroes, like Gilgamesh and Achilles before them, suffer through to the truth of their humanity and win the consoling prize of human fellowship and compassion. Theirs is an *aristeia* stripped of all divine delusions and bestial perversions, scaled to human tragedy, communal and compassionate. Only with eyes accustomed to the darkness of the times and of the human realm can they be seen to blaze forth like the heroes of old as the best and the bravest of men.

94

We have already traced the near obliteration of Heracles which left him prostrate in confusion and despair, surrounded by his bloody handiwork. This man was once as near as any to being a god. He had pressed the bestial border as well. His own eyes peering out out from under the head of a lion in whose skin he was wrapped, he would have been mistaken for a beast if not for a god. Nonetheless, he is now clear and unequivocal regarding his undiluted human lineage. "I own you, not Zeus, to be my father," [1265] he says to the aged Amphitryon. It is his naked humanity which he covers now in shame. Left to himself he will never rise, never uncover and accept his fragile and flawed nature. The chorus of old men, who like the chorus in the *Alcestis* were never so privileged as to imagine themselves other than as they are, anticipate the event about to occur. "When a man's dragging steps quit and he goes down," they sing as they make their own weary way, "he is to be lifted to his feet." [124-125] And that is precisely what we come now to witness.

The entry of Theseus into the human hell unveiled on stage reflects the mythical descent of Heracles into Hades, as well as the heroic entrance of Heracles into the hellishly murderous lair of the demonic usurper Lycus. Each of these represents an image of heroism. The splendors which Heracles displays, however, both in Hades and in the court of Thebes, are inhuman, one moment superhuman and the next moment subhuman. The larger than life Heracles is indomitable but likewise untamed. With or without the ministry of Iris and stage-Madness, Heracles is out of control, metaphysically undefined, living in categorical confusion and strewing a corresponding chaos wherever he goes. Thus, despite his intent to enter as a saving *daimon*, he proves a slaughterous demon, fulfilling rather than thwarting the threats of Lycus. In sharp contrast to Heracles, Theseus is transparently grounded in his humanity and brings to the service of Heracles powers peculiar to human beings: forgiveness, fellowship, and love. The final episode focused on Theseus and Heracles, like book twenty-four of the *Iliad* focused on Priam and Achilles, is to be seen as still another *aristeia*, radically unconventional and yet utterly archaic, the consummate blazing-forth of human glory, such as it is in the unflattering light of truth.

What Theseus brings to Heracles is no escape nor immunity from his suffering, but rather companionship in that suffering. "I have come," he explains to Heracles' father, "to suffer with him." [1203] Theseus ignores Heracles' desperate cries and gestures, warning of pollution. "Among friends," Theseus reassures him, "there is no such thing as pollution." [1234] To Heracles' despairing protestations that he is already past the limit of endurance and will embrace death rather than reenter the human realm, Theseus answers that these are the words of an *epituchon* [1248], an ordinary man, the kind of fellow you would expect to find anywhere, without even trying. They are not the words of a hero. Thus Theseus challenges Heracles to a new heroism, a peculiarly human heroism, whose demands neither gods nor beasts can comprehend or meet. Heracles is asked to endure lucidly the shame of his unspeakable deeds, and to reenter the community of mortals, no longer as a would-be god or beast, no longer as an intimidating, unapproachable power, but as a human being, no more, no less, and no other. Surely we must keep in mind here that this challenge is being spoken out to the citizens of Athens, the savior-city turned tyrant, more slaughterous than salvific, whose atrocities are accumulating at its feet.

Each line in this stunning last episode of the *Heracles* bears commentary and contemplation, which, however, it cannot receive here. Instead, we must leave the *Heracles* with several simple images etched in our minds. The first is that of Heracles weeping. Like Gilgamesh, by his own admission, he has never wept before. His legendary labors, he says, were nothing compared to this. They were relatively easy. The second image is that of Theseus helping Heracles to his feet, which is to say helping him to assume the simple, upright posture of a human being; for this is what he finds so difficult to accept, the yoke of humanity. What makes this bearable is the giving and receiving of another yoke, the yoke of friendship, the yoke of love [*zeugos philion* [1403]. This, then, is the last image, that of Heracles with his arm on Theseus' shoulder, the two of them yoked in compassion and love, as Theseus exits with Heracles in tow, like one of the little boats, one of the little children, whom Heracles the mythical hero had swamped instead of saving.

A moment similarly bright with human truth occurs in the last episode of the *Hippolytus*, when the shredded, battered, blood-sodden Hippolytus is carried home and laid at his father's feet. Hippolytus' pain is equalled only by his father's, whose soul, tangled in the traceries of grief and remorse, has been dragged likewise mercilessly close to death, which is near enough at this moment to make the gods flee. These two once so deluded and pretentious men only now accept their humanity, because it is all they have left; and, alone with it, they draw upon its peculiar grace. They embrace; and Hippolytus, in an act so miraculously improbable that it must be the work of human freedom, forgives Theseus for cursing him so blindly and so effectively. He forgives Theseus for taking the only life he was ever given and will ever have. There is nothing more he, or any mortal, could ever do, which Theseus acknowledges when he says: "how noble a son you have proven yourself to be!" [1452] Here again we are given an Euripidean *aristeia*, a glimpse of humanity at its best.

BEASTS

The human realm must be defined and secured not only over against the gods but also over against the beasts. In fifth-century Greece, the human realm was thought to have crystallized in the polis. Thus the human realm and the political realm were understood as ideally one. In the admiring gaze of its citizens, we might add, Athens was seen to represent the consummate development of the polis. Beasts, like gods, were excluded from the human fellowship of this and of any other Greek city, though beasts, made to nod their head in assent before the blade, "willingly" spilled their blood on the city's altars, mostly set off in the *temene* of the gods. Political fellowship is rooted in *philia*, loving friendship, the bond of the polis; and friendship requires essential equality. Friends, and thus fellow-citizens, are to hold all things, at least all essential things, in common. The suffering of a friend makes one suffer; and the joy of a friend makes one joyous. The boundaries between friends, in short, are permeable; and, while retaining their own individual identities, friends become one. In theory, all fellow-citizens are friends, while cities, on the other hand, may well be fierce enemies. Euripides, as has been noted already and will be explored further, would extend the consortium of the city to the consortium of humankind, lest the unity

97

forged within disparate cities be used to divide and ravage the community of mortals.

Between humans and beasts, however, there can be no final friendship; for they lack fundamental equality and commonality. In prehistoric times, the predatory power of beasts was broken by the conspiracy of human strength and wit. Beasts became prey, the preferable object of human aggression and a staple of human nutrition. Once their power was broken, the "otherness" of beasts made possible their victimization. As quarry for the hunt, as victims for sacrifice, and as meat for the feast, beasts obliged human fellowship without any hope of sharing in it. Their inhumanity is decisive and immutable. Though the beasts share with mortals the essential limitation of death, they seem not to be haunted by death. They do not live with death as a companion but only confront it in extremity. Mortals, on the other hand, can and do on occasion lie before an open fire after a grand feast, walled in and roofed securely from any conceivable threat, and, despite youth and health and wealth, shake with terror and dread at the mere thought of their finitude. For mortals, life is not precarious only when it is at immediate risk. Rather, for mortals, life is essentially precarious. Beasts require the literal, sensorily apprehended presence of danger for their hairs to bristle, their eyes to dilate, their hearts to pound, and so on. For all of this and more to beset them, mortals require no more than imagination. And this imagination, elusive as it may be, suffices to open a chasm between mortals and their otherwise fellow-animals, the beasts.

Although the literal tooth-and-claw primacy of the beasts was wrested from them in prehistoric times, they retained considerable symbolic power and eminence in the imaginations of the ancient poets and artists and, we may presume, of those ancients who have left no lasting record of their obsessions. As symbols, beasts, except when consciously anthropomorphized, always represented inhumanity and thus extremity; for the bestial, however it is imagined, lies invariably beyond some boundary of the human. From the human vantage-point, the denizens of the inhuman realm tended to fuse. Otherness is otherness, or so it must have seemed; for, as depicted poetically and iconographically, beasts and gods were often strangely bonded. For that matter, within the political order, wherein the human sphere is conventionally constricted to encompass only

98

fellow-citizens or political allies to the exclusion of women, barbarians, slaves, and enemies, outsiders were imaginatively de-humanized and likened to beasts in preparation for their being actually violated. At the present moment, however, our focus is upon the metaphysical realm, wherein the multivalent symbolic power of beasts will be made more clear by reference to several examples from Greek literature and art.

Both literary and iconographic evidence suggests that the imaginatively preeminent beast in ancient Egypt and the Middle East, as well as in Greece from the Bronze Age into the classical period, was the lion. This suggestion bears even more weight if we accept that the Gorgon is originally and essentially leonine. From Gilgamesh to Euripides, from pre-dynastic Egyptian palettes to the lions-gate of Mycenae, from Heracles to Achilles to Dionysus to Alexander the Great, the lion remains a symbol of awesome, almost divine, power, sometimes lordly and benign, sometimes utterly savage. A lesser beast and thus a lesser symbol is the dog, a symbol of snarling, vicious, small-scale ferocity, as well as of the impurity of battle. In the *Iliad*, Teucer calls Hector a *kuna lussetera*, a rabid dog, a warrior gone beserk, so beside himself that he forgets any reverence for gods or fellow-mortals. Leaping to the fifth-century, sooner or later, Sophocles likens every one of his heroes to one beast or another; and Euripides too employs a kaleidoscopic bestiary to imagine his characters and their deeds.

Rather than catalogue further the bestial images in Greek literature and art, we would do well to consider more closely in a specifically Euripidean context the two bestial symbols already noted, the lion and the dog, while adding a third, the deer; for in these three we may comprehend the spectrum of bestial symbols employed by Euripides to illuminate their corresponding human possibilities. This spectrum is primarily one of power and weakness and resembles that proposed by Thrasymachus in the *Republic*. At one extreme is near-absolute, unaccountable power, represented by the lion; and at the other extreme is near-absolute weakness, represented by the deer. Absolute power and absolute weakness are inhuman, the one being humanly unattainable and the other being humanly unnecessary. Only gods, whose sovereign otherness may be symbolized by beasts, possess and exercise unqualified power; and only beasts, particularly the hapless, harmless victims of sacrifice, display weakness unqualified by moral defiance. Mortals are always only would-be gods and would-be beasts, never capable of rising to unconditional power and yet always capable of rising above unconditional weakness.

First, we consider the dream of absolute power, the unaccountable power of the tyrant, symbolized by the lion. In Euripides' *Phoenician Women*, we witness the struggle of two brothers, Eteocles and Polyneices, the cursed sons of Oedipus, for such power. They are likened in their hideous, fratricidal struggle to "twin beasts" [1296] and to lions [1573]. The prize for which they contend and over which they soon slaughter each other is avowed with shocking candor by Eteocles in these words to his mother, Jocasta [503-506]:

> Mother, with you I will mince no words.
> I would outreach the stars,
> Run the circuit of the sun,
> Harrow the haunts of hell,
> If I could do this one thing: grasp tyranny,
> Tyranny the greatest of the gods.

It is utterly clear to Eteocles' lucidly perverted soul that only two possibilities exist for him, as for his brother: to be a tyrant or to be a slave - to be a lion, lordly and ruthlessly savage, or to be an ox, a beast of burden, yoked to another's will and ever ready for his blade. The diseased divinity in whose malignant service each individual must be mutated into either a master or a slave is noted and named by Jocasta as *philotimia* [532], the overweening desire to excel and so to win universal deference. Jocasta's decrying of *philotimia* as the most perverse of daimonic forces and as devoid of justice represents a lonely voice not only within the poetic tradition but also within imperial Athens; for *philotimia* provided not only the foundation of traditional heroism but also the motivation of contemporary empire. Jocasta explains how *philotimia* invariably leaves behind it a trail of devastation and death. Instead, she would have her sons honor equality [*isotēs*,536], the fair bond of friends and of cities, whose legacy is stability and peace. Like Crestes and Medea, however, Eteocles would rather drag his house to ruin than suffer the slightest diminishment. An addict to his own ambition, he is blind to the space between everything and nothing. He must have either one or the other, which he does; but not before spilling rivers of innocent blood.

Medea too spills innocent blood en-route to near-divine power. She, of course, shines dark and triumphant at the close of her drama, appearing in the machine like a goddess. True to her threats, she manifests herself as a *daimon*, quite equal to the work of rewarding her friends and wreaking chaos on her enemies. Described in the opening episode as a lioness [187] by her children's nurse, she is in the final episode described by the undone Jason as "not a woman at all but a lioness with a nature more bestial than Tyrrhenian Scylla." [1342-1343] In this last moment of the play, perched in that place reserved in Attic tragedy for the gods, she is inhuman and thus momentarily exempt from the limits of mortality though not from the excesses of bestiality.

Plummeting now to the nethermost point on the spectrum of human power and weakness, we come to the slave and the victim, symbolized by the beast of burden and the sacrifical victim. The fate of the slave and that of the victim would appear to be incomparably disparate, as disparate as life and death. Indeed, they are just that; but the life of the slave constitutes a living death, a daily approximation of death. The victim Polyxena, in the *Hecuba*, torn from between her mother's knees like the trembling doe in Hecuba's dream, is made to spill out her blood all at once on the tomb of Achilles. This is the fate which Polyxena prefers, in no uncertain terms, to the daily death of the slave, in which life is spilled out slowly like wasted wine dripping from a cracked cup. This much Polyxena makes quite clear to Odysseus, whom she says she will make to effort to resist(349-368).

> I was born a princess.
> I was nursed on the highest of hopes,
> > to be a bride for kings, vying for my hand,
> > to be the queen of the best among them,
> > to live to a full age in his court.
> I grew to be the acknowledged mistress
> > of Troy's girls and women,
> > conspicuous in every respect.
> Mortality aside,
> > I was a goddess.

And now I am a slave.
The name alone, so alien in every way,
    is enough to enamor me of death.
Am I to be an item for sale to coarse men,
    I, the sister of Hector,
    sister to the princes of Troy?
Am I to know only harsh necessity,
    sweeping some man's floors,
    kneading his bread,
    from one weary day to the next?
Am I, the bride of kings,
    to let some crude slave from god knows where
    defile me in his filthy bed?
Never!
I will take one last look at freedom
    and consign myself to hell.

Polyxena's subsequent speech at the grave of Achilles, related to Hecuba by Talthybius, is surely one of the most stirring speeches in ancient tragedy. This young girl shames the leering mob of Troy-sacking Greeks with her bold, defiant courage. She cries out for her hands to be untied so that she might die as she has lived, a proud, free woman and no man's slave. She bares her breasts, leans back her head, and spews her one, only life across the earthen mound piled over the corpse of the greatest of the Greeks. In all this, Polyxena's literal defeat is not in question; for she is dead. Neither is her moral victory in the slightest question; for she outshines the amassed Greek army and their corrupt fame. Hers is an inextinguishable beauty; while they are for all time common butchers.

Similarly, in the *Iphigeneia in Aulis*, the decision before Iphigeneia is not whether to live or to die, but simply how to die. She cannot hope to take on and to overwhelm the entire Greek army. Instead, she can either be dragged off to her death like some squalling, netted beast or she can go to her death freely, as did Polyxena, with as much dignity as defeat permits. Bestial victims are always either unwitting or unwilling or both. Not so human victims, who, utterly emptied of hope, may lucidly accept their death with humor or bravado or grace, as did Socrates or Polyxena or Iphigeneia. Nowhere, perhaps, is the resemblance between humans and beasts more inescapable than in death; for they live and thus lose a common life. It is equally true, however, that nowhere is the difference between humans and beasts more dramatically evident than in witting, willing death, such as that of Iphigeneia.

Deceived by her own father into thinking that she awaits the hand and the bed of Achilles, Iphigeneia and her mother prepare for the wedding sacrifice. When she learns that she is the sacrifice and that Agamemnon, not Achilles, will make her bleed her virginal blood, not in a wedding bed but upon an altar, Iphigeneia's instinct is to plead for her life and to elude her fate at whatever price. So long as she imagines her fate to be alterable, she will endeavor to alter it. Soon, however, she sees that she is not merely in danger but, indeed, doomed. The perception of her unconditional weakness leads her to a peculiarly human insight and resolve. In resisting she will only herself slide from human grace and squander other precious lives. Instead, she wills what is willed and thus usurps the power of those who would take her life from her. She will not be alienated from her own death or in her own death. Her death belongs to her as inalienably as does her life and she will undertake it in her own way. "Hear me, mother," she says to Clytemnestra, "hear what has occured to me and what I have in mind to do" [1374-1376]:

> I have imagined my death
> and all is well.
> Now I want to do it right.
> I want to shine when I die.
> I want nothing to do
> with anything craven or cheap.

And shine she does, as her father, the king of kings, never managed to do, before or since. She was led to expect a marriage; so it is a marriage she will announce and embrace. She is to be the bride of Hellas. There will be no tears, no black veils; only the wedding crown and joyous song. Then, in one shuddering moment, when the sacrificial scream replaces the love-cry, she will thrill her spouse and leave him bereft, to mourn her forever. Iphigeneia enters freely now into the sordid pretense created by her shabby father to cover his own cowardice and ambition; and she expands it into myth. She turns a lie into a legend. She, not her father, and not

103

the mob he pretends to lead, shall be the Savior of Greece. She will be the best thing about the war in this its finest moment, so far as it reflects on her. So far as it reflects on the army and the non-entities who command them, however, this is the war's darkest moment, its most damning atrocity.

However one assesses the authenticity and interprets the meaning of Artemis' final sleight of hand in substituting for Iphigeneia, as the blade descends, a young hind, the image of Iphigeneia as archetypal human victim endures. The status of no truth within the human realm is altered by the miraculous intervention of Artemis, though the reputation of Artemis may be appreciably improved thereby. From the human, ethical perspective, however, it would be no different if Agamemnon had closed his eyes and accidentily missed his mark. Like the veiled girl in the *Alcestis*, the arrival of the surrogate deer occurs too late to change anything essential; for the truth has already been glimpsed. And the audience must live with the truth, whether or not Alcestis and Iphigeneia are granted poetic reprieves.

The third and final bestial symbol we will consider here is that of the dog, which lies mid-way between the ravaging lion and the ravaged deer in the spectrum of human power and weakness. The dog, virtually indistinguishable at times from the wolf, is savage and resourceful, but hardly sovereign. It is most intimidating in its plural form, when roaming in packs, and is irresistible only briefly when it is beside itself, rabid with rage. The dog is neither invulnerable nor without recourse. It can inflict pain, even death; but not without suffering its own share of pain in turn.

Clearly there are many such "dogs" in the corpus of Euripidean drama, resigned to suffer but resolved to inflict suffering as well. Briefly - for this current discussion has already taken us across into the political order - we will consider the broken but effectual queen of Troy in the *Hecuba*. Hecuba is living proof, and knows as much, that weakness as well as power corrupts. Suffering brings wisdom; but excessive suffering, endured past the point of personal endurance, is disfiguring and brings not wisdom but evil genius. Hecuba longs to die before she becomes as dark as all that has been done to her; but Zeus will not let her go. Instead, with merciless largesse, he seals her every crack as if she were the last vessel in his fleet. Finally, she is consumed with a single desire, to see a bit of justice done; but neither the powers above nor the powers below will lift a finger or give a fig for justice. So she will do a bit of justice herself, poetic justice, or, in a word, revenge, which she accomplishes through a combination of wit and collective rage. She herself, however, has sustained wounds as deep as any she inflicts; and her end is not what would be described as kind. Transformed literally into a mad dog, she will climb the mast of a Greek ship and plunge to her death.

Women are, indeed, frequently likened to dogs in Greek poetry. In the Greek imagination, they are weak unless they are frenzied and united. As Hecuba points out to Agamemnon, however, the power of women evokes wonder and dread as soon as it is gathered and focused. Furthermore, she says, it proves irresistible if it ever be combined with cunning. Women, like Polyxena and Iphigeneia, are indeed Greek hunters' prey, marked victims, so long as they are alone; but, as soon as they claim their collective power and release the fury within them and employ their considerable guile, they take up their own hunt and track their own prey.

What is as critical as it is obvious is that the lion, the deer, and the dog are all beasts; and the human possibilities glimpsed in them are likewise bestial. They find their way into Euripidean drama, presumably, because they find their way into our lives; and Euripides was committed, as we know, to presenting life as it is in fact lived. Neither their occurence nor the frequency of their occurence in Euripides' plays can be construed fairly as indicating Euripides' personal approval. If I may venture a Euripidean judgement in this matter, it seems that human beings do best to see themselves and their possibilities, as did Gilgamesh and Enkidu, Achilles and Priam, Heracles and Theseus: in each other.

IV. THE POLITICAL ORDER

Within the metaphysical order, or simply the cosmos, human being is distinguished from divine being and from bestial being. Human beings, defined by their mortality, stand at an essential remove both from the deathless lucidity of gods and from the deathful oblivion of beasts. Within the metaphysical order, human being is essentially one, admitting of no particular exemptions nor privileges. Even the sons of the gods, recalling a choral verse from the *Alcestis*, go dark in death. Kings, slaves, Greeks, barbarians, women and warriors meet, on the far side of death, with the same undiscriminating obliteration. On the near side of death, however, within the political order, or more simply the polis, human being is divided into these and many other denominations. The seamless consortium of mortals is, in the city, shredded into tatters until man and woman, rich and poor, master and slave, citizen and stranger are all but unrecognizable to each other in their common humanity. Indeed, they are often left to wonder whether they have anything at all in common with each other. Screened by convention, the natural solidarity of the doomed is replaced by a spectral scheme of privilege and oppression enforced by prejudice and wilfulness.

The Greek theatre, as we have seen already, was a place of essential disclosure, wherein the truth of humanity was laid bare for common contemplation and acknowledgment. Metaphysical insight, however, is all too easily shadowed and compromised by political corruption. The essential unity of humankind, an undeniable corollary of mortality, must be argued afresh in the political realm, wherein it is the least evident of truths. In fact, the political order appears premised upon its denial. The political order, the specifically human realm, which ought to contradict the hierarchical structure of the metaphysical order, mostly mimics it instead. Characteristically, within the political order, one human being or human faction would play the god to others and, time and power permitting, would reduce the rest of humankind to bestial servitude and instrumentality. In short, the truth glimpsed briefly and brilliantly in the metaphysical realm perishes at once of its own impracticality in the political realm.

The timeless argument for the necessary and natural corruption of the political realm is nowhere stated more lucidly than in the *Republic* of Plato, wherein Thrasymachus argues that every human being strives naturally and necessarily for the absolute power and freedom of a god at the inevitable expense of every other human being's similar striving. Every good corresponding to every human desire is, so far as Thrasymachus knows and argues, fundamentally unshareable, a maddening fact made all the worse by the infinitude of human desire. Consequently, one man's happiness means everyone else's hell; and only the tyrant, whose will has its own way always, is truly happy. Thrasymachus, however, knew well that compromise is unavoidable and collusion best. Tyranny is less dangerous and more practicable when pursued collectively, which insight was foundational for Athenian imperialism, as for every form of imperialism before or since. The brazen claims of the Athenian generals at Melos, as reported by Thucydides, propound the same cynical doctrine. In fact, as noble a soul as Pericles saw less and less wrong with tyranny the more inclusive it became of the Athenian polis. Tyranny blown large to the scale of the city was no longer something despicable but was, instead, seen as simple destiny.

In the drama of Euripides, however, we glimpse a political order radically consistent with the essential human truths perceived within the metaphysical order, a political order purged of divine pretense and bestial demeanment. This is not to say that Euripides founded an actual city, any more than did Plato in the *Republic*. What may be found within the dramas of Euripides, as within the dialogues of Plato, is a city without walls, a city raised in thought and speech alone, inhabitable only for the imagination and the heart, a spiritual haunt wherein moral outrage and defiance might echo and resound. The facts, after all, are on the side of Thrasymachus; but facts are sometimes the enemy of truth. The fact that the political realm seemingly always has been and likely will remain an arena for human competition and conflict rather than the site of human recognition and communion constitutes a human scandal not a human truth. Against this scandal Euripides and others raise their voices in defiance; but, admittedly, such voices are never so many nor so powerful

108

as to bring down the walls of the cities they despise or to raise up the walls of the cities they envision.

Nevertheless, moral protest against the corruption of the established political order may be seen to constitute a refutation of the truthfulness, if not the actuality, of that order. After all, the consummately arrogant Athenian generals at Melos and the grotesquely belligerent Thrasymachus of the *Republic* not only flexed their muscle but propounded a doctrine. In their arrogance they claimed to possess not only clout but also the truth. In short, their claim came down to this: all human distinctions, even moral distinctions between justice and injustice, decency and degeneracy, are reducible to the singular distinction between power and weakness. Naturally and necessarily, they would claim, the powerful exploit their power and the weak acquiesce in their weakness. The irony is that the Melians in their weakness did no such thing. They failed utterly to observe what the Athenian generals and Thrasymachus propounded to be a law of nature; and such exceptions to the would-be rule may be said to cast into doubt if not into disrepute the truth of the Athenian claim. At the very least it may be said that the moral outcome of the Melian campaign was a good deal more ambiguous than the military outcome, in which the Melian defeat was total.

Before we consider the many faces and voices of political defiance and protest in Euripidean drama, we must complicate the too simplistic image of the Athenian political order so far presented in this chapter. Without denying that Athens deserved its title as the "tyrant city," it must be pointed out that city-scale tyranny is at least two-faced and thus shows a very different side to those within the circle of its favor from that which it shows to those without. On the one hand, Athens was for most of the fifth century a democracy, a kingless city governed by the principle of *isonomia*, the equality of all citizens in making and administering the law. Political order was likened to cosmic order; and both were seen to depend upon equality. *Isonomia*, oneness before the law, and *homonoia*, oneness of mind, were seen to be the conceptual pillars of democracy; and their realization had been the slow work of centuries, in which the power of families and factions was broken and reconstituted as the common possession of all citizens. Viewed from within its walls and through the eyes of one of its own sons, Athens might well seem to be, as it was and is often seen, the guarantor of a quality of life rarely glimpsed by others and the watershed in man's trek from

109

savagery to civilization. We sense the rightful pride Euripides himself may well have taken in the extent of *isonomia* in his mother-city, when in the *Suppliant Women* [403-408] we hear Theseus correct the Theban herald who has asked to speak with Athens' master [*tyrannos*], as if Athens, like so many other cities were a city of slaves:

> Stranger, you are already off on the wrong foot,
>   looking for a master in this place.
> This city is not under one man's rule.
> It is free.
> Here the people govern, taking their turns,
>   in yearly succession.
> Power in this place is not handed over to the rich.
> The poor have as much power as anyone else.

Athenian democracy may be said to have reached its consummate form in the vision and era of Pericles, in which the city and the cosmos became fused or, more accurately, confused. The cosmos was collapsed into the city, *phusis* into *nomos*. In this scheme of things, an Athenian was born first and foremost to Athens, which nourished and nurtured his life and thus possessed a primal claim upon it. The collective self, the civic "we," eclipsed the individual self. The collective mind and will of Athens usurped the potential tyrant within each citizen and were crystallized into an absolute political entity not unlike the leviathan of Hobbes, who clearly did more than translate Thucydides. What was central both to Hobbes' leviathan and to Pericles' Athens was the power and prerogative of collective human passion, will, and speech to define reality. For both Pericles and Hobbes, *nomos*, the collective assertion of will, is absolute, or rather as absolute as is the power which inflicts it upon the world. Law is nothing other than collective self-assertion; and the city is the engine behind it.

The issues raised in this present discussion are admittedly complex and seemingly obscure. They come down, however, to something quite simple and pointed. What Euripides witnessed in his own city was the creation of a radically secular state, secular to its core, no matter how girdled it might have been with pieties. The official gods of the Athenian polis in the fifth century were tame, household pets. They blessed its troops and sanctioned its edicts when and as they were told to do so. In such a regime, the metaphysical order is overturned and

110

human beings, at least those coalesced into the collective tyranny, lord it over all of existence indiscriminately. There are only facts, no truths; and these facts are the ephemeral products of force. There is no such thing, for instance, as human being, poised precariously between and sharing a cosmos with bestial and divine being, except perhaps as a poetic or philosophical figure of speech. In the place of the human being there is the citizen, identified and defined by civil law; and, in the place of the rest of the cosmos - human, bestial, or divine - there is otherness, whose status is in principle at the capricious discretion of the city. In short, there is, on the one hand, the "we" and, on the other, the "they" or even the "it." If we lay bare the theoretical core of Athenian imperial policy, that is what we find.

If one were an Athenian citizen and equipped with neither imagination nor conscience, then one might see nothing amiss, much less appalling, in Athenian imperial theory and practice. However, if one were, for instance, a woman, a slave, or a barbarian, then it would require neither imagination nor conscience to notice that something outrageous was in the air. If justice is, in simplest terms, respect for the nature of anyone or anything and injustice the violation of that nature, then what was in the air was injustice. The political order, as envisioned by and embodied in imperial Athens, denied the humanity of all but its citizens, whose humanity it all the same disfigured. In Euripidean drama, we hear as frequently as if it were a refrain the denial of that denial and thus the affirmation of a common humanity without disfigurement.

The political order envisioned by Euripides and embodied in his plays seeks above all to be just, namely to respect the truth of human nature as discerned within the metaphysical order. The truth of human nature is violated as soon as some human beings fancy themselves as would-be gods and set out to reduce others to would-be beasts. Both cosmic justice and political justice lie in affirming the radical inequality of human being with every other being and the radical equality of every individual human being with every other individual human being. Thus the truth of the political order lies in its transparency to the truth of the metaphysical order. Jocasta sees and says precisely this to her raving son Eteocles; but he is blind to her vision and deaf to her words [*Phoenecian Women*,528ff]:

> Eteocles, my son,
> The legacy of age is not all bad.

111

With experience can come words
    wiser than those of youth.
Child,
    why do you strive for a place above others?
Such striving is, of all possessing powers,
    the most perverse.
Stop this.
The divinity you worship is injustice...
Better to honor equality,
    the bond of friends, of cities, of allies.
It is the nature of equality
        to stand up steady and strong
        in the human circle.

Jocasta proceeds to explain to her hapless son that in the absence of equality, enmity is sown, the lesser hating the greater. The contrasting harmony we witness in the cosmos is the fruit of equality, night yielding to day and day to night, neither begrudging the other its due. Not so with her sons. "You think having more than your share is better?" Jocasta asks her son bitterly and futilely; "but what you think has nothing behind it." [553]

Within the essential equality of the human realm, however, Euripides was a keen observer of human differences. No one could with any grounds argue that the differences, for example, between youth and age, high birth and low birth, or freedom and servitude were lost on him. What he questioned was not the existence but the final significance of such distinctions. A good many of life's capricious privileges would seem to be contained in noble birth; and yet the significance of noble birth is commonly discounted in Euripidean drama, as in the following choral fragment from the lost *Alexander* [fr.52]:

Among us mortals,
Words poured out in praise of noble birth
Are idle and excessive.
Long ago, when we were first spawned,
When the earth our mother brought us forth,
There was no telling us apart,
As the earth had made us.
Apart from what we had in common,

We had nothing.
Those born into high places
And those born well beneath them
Are still one family, one seed.
The voice of the city [*nomos*],
Has conspired with time,
To proclaim birth to the right parents
A matter of pride.

High birth is, in Euripidean drama, a matter of irrelevance. It is nobility of spirit that matters. "Of noble birth," we read in the *Dictys* [fr.336], "I have little good to say. To my eyes, the good man is the man of high birth; and the rogue, even if he comes from better stock than Zeus himself, is the one basely born." It does not take Euripides to go on to note that those nobly born have no peculiar claim or head-start on decency. In fact, we find in a fragment from the *Antigone* [fr.55] the claim that "the misdeeds of the rich are many." At the very least, what we fail to find in Euripides' plays, and perhaps anywhere else for that matter, is any correspondence between privilege and decency. In Euripidean drama, the wealthy, the high-born, the powerful, the beautiful, the city's "best and brightest," for all their giftedness, seldom display a corresponding moral grandeur. Rather, they tend to lead shallow, shabby lives at best and blind, savage lives at worst. More often than not in Euripidean drama, it is a slave, a child, a barbarian, a woman, one of the obscured or oppressed, who shines. The only inequality that finally matters to Euripides, it seems, is ethical; and, in the familiar words of Flannery O'Connor, "a good man is hard to find," which more or less sums up the following complaint of Orestes in the *Electra* [368ff]:

There is no driven path to excellence of soul;
    for the race of mortals are an unruly lot.
I have seen eminent fathers raise worthless sons,
    and stalwart sons come from sheer corruption.
Within the souls of wealthy men,
    I have glimpsed gnawing hunger,
    while in bodies lacking almost everything,
    I have found a profound grasp of things.
So how, I ask, are we to sort through our race
    and find the truly good man?

113

What measure might we use?
Wealth?... Poverty?... Daring in battle?...
Best to ignore measures such as these,
and put them far from our thoughts.

Even without a rule of thumb for ferreting them out in advance, it remains evident on the Euripidean stage that some lives are more just than others in that they they are lived out with greater respect for the natures of all beings, while other lives trample and disfigure everything in their path. Neither the essential equality of all human beings, nor the inscrutable source of their ethical inequality, renders all human lives morally equivalent. The integrity of each life lies cupped like water in each one's hands. No one and nothing else beyond the individual is finally accountable for whether it is lost or not. Nobility or baseness of spirit emerges from deep within the life and reveals its core, its singular truth or falsity. Every other distinction is imposed from without, whether by chance or fate or human caprice, and hangs on a life like a garment. "Those who seem to all appearances to be utterly glorious," rails Andromache, "are below the surface like everyone else." [*Andromache*,330-331] Apart from inward differences, differences of spirit, what divides one human being from another is essentially negligible. "A minute sliver of gold buys a man's daily bread," explains the peasant husband of Electra, "and on a full stomach, the poor man and the rich man are virtually equal." [*Electra*,429-431]

In a fragment from Euripides' *Antigone* [fr.168], we read that "the only thing contemptible about a bastard is his name. In his nature he is the equal of the legitimate son." Within the Euripidean corpus we find similar comments on the names, for example, of "slave" and "barbarian." To say, however, that nothing more powerful or pernicious than names cleaves and classifies humanity into more categories than anyone can count is not to say anything remotely reassuring; for *nomos* or law is the very structure of the city and *nomos* is nothing more than words or names. In this context, to name something is to assign to it its parochial nature, to "coin" its meaning and value as if it were a piece of raw metal waiting to be stamped into currency. What is in a name? Within the city, everything. Like masks over the souls of those who bear them, the names of "woman," "slave," and "barbarian" suffice to obscure the humanity possessed in common with free, Greek, men and to justify the

114

discounting of their lives; and so the truth of the political order, human equality, dies myriad deaths.

WOMEN

There is perhaps no more revealing an entry into the discussion of women in ancient Greece than that provided by even a brief consideration of the very words most commonly used to denote "woman," a feminine mortal. If we set aside *kore* and *graus*, which denote a woman before and after her child-bearing years, respectively, the most common word for woman was *gune*, which literally and not surprisingly means "childbearer." Clearly the central and most respectable function of woman was seen to be the bearing of legitimate children, most especially sons, for which a woman had also to be a wife. Thus *gune* may also mean "wife" or "mate," even a bestial mate. The word which in poetic diction specifically denoted a man's wife was *damar*, literally "the tamed or subdued one." *Damar* is derived from *damao*, which means to tame, to yoke, to subdue, to enslave, to rape, or to kill. The *damar* is the object of all of these activities; and, indeed, women and wives knew their share of each.

This confusion of women with beasts and slaves, embedded in the language, pervades the literature of ancient Greece as well. In the *Iliad*, for example, when warriors taunt and threaten each other, their words most often aim to turn the opponent into a woman or a beast. In the *Theogony* of Hesiod, women appear late on the human scene as a *genos* or race apart, a *kakon* or "evil thing" fashioned by Zeus, the implement of his revenge on mortal men for their possession of stolen divine fire. Adorned and garlanded by Athena, this *kakon* becomes *kalon* or lovely to behold, all but irresistible to men. Inhuman, guileful, neither to be resisted nor endured, woman - the *kalon kakon*, the "beguiling perversity" - brings an end to man's primeval well-being. Similarly, in *Works and Days*, the phantasy of an originally womanless world, uncursed with toil and evil, is shattered by the arrival of woman, this time with a name, Pandora, a bane on all men. Woman, with her insatiable appetite for food and sex, consigns men to a life of labor, that is to the ploughing of virgin soil and to the sowing of seed. Woman, in short, is a

115

divinely set trap, a divinely fragranced beast. In the seventh century, the Aegean poet Semonides, no more a friend to women than was Hesiod, traced the perverse characters of women to the beasts where in his view they presumably belonged. Beyond Hesiod and Semonides, women were quite commonly likened to bees, sometimes favorably with a nod to their industriousness, sometimes disparagingly, with drones in mind.

Even a glancing consideration of ancient Greek art confirms the claim that women were commonly imagined in inhuman categories. Images of war, hunting, athletics, sex, and sacrifice may be said to dominate Greek pictorial art; and it may further be argued that all of these spheres of activity were tangled and entwined in the Greek imagination. The common bond between them is violence. It is surely a commonplace by now to point out that from the stone age spear to the most advanced ballistic missle, man's weapons represent him sexually, as it is to point out that athletic contests, ancient and modern, are more or less benign battles. We have already discussed the diversion of violence from human victims to bestial ones, and the consecration of such killing in sacrifice. Aristotle likens the first menstrual flow of a young maiden to the flow of blood from a slaughtered victim, though the likeness between the first blood shed by a victim on the altar and the first blood shed by a wife in bed is more commonly explored in Greek literature. Further, the ritual *sphage*, the sacrifical slaughter of animals immediately before battle, in the face of one's enemies, to be consummated not in a meal but in battle, clearly anticipates the letting of human blood to follow. In rare instances, the *sphagia*, the blood victims, may have been human; and there is perhaps no more poignant symbol or expression of the renunciation of life and of sexuality entailed in mortal combat than the sacrifice of a virgin, a theme familiar to Euripides. Even if the bed of love and the field of battle represented distinct aspirations, reflected in the distinct figures of Paris and Achilles, their corresponding activities shared a common word, *mignumi*, "to mingle with," whether in combat or in copulation.

Even these few brush strokes, as it were, convey a sense of the image and the place of woman in ancient Greece. Now, in order to bring into sharper focus the immediate context for Euripides' concerns with women, we turn pointedly to fifth-century Athens, with whose legendary founding various tales of virgin-sacrifice were connected. From the outset it is instructive to reflect upon Athena, who gave more than her name to her city. Athena, though a feminine deity, is no friend of women. In fact, she has precious nothing to do with women at all. Sprung from

116

the axed head of her father Zeus, she is motherless, while as declared virgin, she is likewise childless. Motherhood, the common experience and raison d'etre of all respectable Athenian women, is utterly foreign to her. She is a warrior, born in full armor from the skull of her father. In her most famed embodiment, the statue of Athena Parthenos crowning the Athenian acropolis, she was stripped of any semblance of womanhood and bore not only the emblems of Athenian militarism but the emblem of Athenian misogyny as well. Depicted on the outside of her shield was the Amazonomachia, the legendary defeat of the Amazons by Theseus, marking the final fracturing of feminine power, while on the inside was depicted the pre-historic defeat of the centaurs by the Lapiths, aboriginal Athenians.

These two myths, borne triumphantly by Athena Parthenos, were utterly foundational for Athens. Together they represented the decisive wresting of power from women, on the one hand, and from beasts, on the other. The only surviving threat to Athenian supremacy were the gods; and they were for the most part either domesticated or disbelieved. The gods survived, of course, and prevailed in myth, concerning which it is telling to point out that Greek mythology is, as everyone knows, suffused with rape, the master-rapist being Zeus, the king of the gods. The conquests of Zeus can hardly be seen as the naughty fruit of celestial lust; for rape, whether Olympian or ordinary, is not about desire but about dominance. In this light, we must admit that Greek mythology, so far from condemning violence towards women, celebrates it. What has not been so commonly known or openly acknowledged is what is only fair to call the phallic obsession of fifth-century Athens. Indeed, if we consider only its phallic processions and drama, its omnipresent herms, and its plethora of bizarre phallic art, we would not be rash in ascribing to Athens a cult of the male generative principle and an adulation of the penis, all having little or nothing to do with love and everything to do with power.

An Athenian woman's claim upon citizenship and her participation in public life were indeed marginal. With certain ritual exceptions, a woman was expected to be as publically silent and unseen as possible. A certian liberation may have accompanied menopause; but this likely meant increased freedom to frequent public places rather than any enhanced part in public affairs. The simple fact that from fifth-century Athens there survives not a single word written by a woman nor, with the possible exception of some vases, a single artefact attributable to a

117

woman's hand is as eloquent as any chapter which may be written on the obscurity of the Athenian woman. Not only were Athenian women inconspicuous; they were officially anonymous as well. A female child's name was not listed in the records of the phratry, i.e. the clan or ward; and the citizenship of a male child was traced through his father and his maternal grandfather, without mention of his mother's name. Just as the wife was commonly seen as housing and nurturing her husband's seed, without contributing anything beyond hospitality to the procreative process, so the mother was seen as the neutral, nameless conduit through which citizenship was passed down from one male generation to the next.

The woman's or wife's sphere of influence was essentially the home, where she bore her children and managed the household's affairs. This is not to say that she was sovereign within the home. Rather, Athenian art, literature, and architecture conspire to tell a domestic story not of female sovereignty but of female solitude and subservience. From such evidence, it would seem that women, as wives, were primarily mothers, water-carriers, and weavers. They were more or less confined to the *gunaikonitis*, the women's quarters, where meals were prepared, children raised, and domestic crafts practiced; in short, where women's lives were mostly lived out. It seems that husband and wife did not ordinarily share the same room or bed. Instead, children were conceived on the *kline*, a narrow couch designed and reserved for intercourse. It may be argued that wives often or even mostly ate their meals separately from their husbands and their grown sons, who lived a masculine life apart in the men's quarters, the *andrones*, usually more ample and adorned than the rest of the house.

Reserving their wives for legitimate offspring, Athenian men regularly entertained *hetairai* or prostitues in the *andron*, the "man's room," a dining-room equipped with couches and located with conveniently direct access to the street. Here the man of the house hosted his symposia, or drinking-feasts, at which his invited male companions were amply provided with food, drink, entertainment, and sex. The tales of many such symposia are graphically told by myriad surviving *kylikes* painted with clearly uncensored scenes familiar to symposia-goers. The *kylix* was a man's cup kept from wives' and children's eyes in the men's quarters and thus an arguably reliable witness to the events occuring therein. Admitting the exceptional moment of mutual tenderness or shared amusement, the larger story told

118

on these cups is one of sexual abuse and humiliation, particularly if we keep in mind the never-pictured but ever-nearby wife, the presumably neither deaf nor unimaginative wife, under whose roof her husband conducted his revels.

There is a favorite fantasy among many classicists of the bright, engaging, free-spirited, fun-loving Athenian prostitute, who was the virtual equal of her male companions. The historical center-post of this fantasy is the famed figure of Aspasia, consort of Pericles, and admittedly no mean figure in her own right. Yet even if Aspasia was as free and influential and self-possessed as she has often been described, an exception tends to prove rather than discount the rule; and the rule for women, whether wives or whores, was arguably closer to the complaint of the chorus of women in the *Thesmophoriazousai* [786-787] who claimed "men without exception attribute to the race of women a host of evils, so that we are regarded as the source and the substance of every evil afflicting men."

Apart from the female protests and partisanship to be found in Euripidean drama, to which we will soon turn, there is to be sure a counter-tradition co-existent with the prevalent misogyny ingrained and evident in Athenian society. Stated more simply, Euripides was not the only friend Athenian women had. First and foremost, they had each other. Even without the numerous surviving references to female solidarity in myth, art, literature, and ritual, we might assume the existence of a female counter-culture, rebellious and resilient. Indeed, in fifth-century Athens, in addition to the clandestine confidences which must have been shared in the women's quarters and at the communal fountain, the yearly festivals of the *Skira* and the *Thesmophoria*, for example, virtually institutionalized the political solidarity of women, while in the *Adonia* and the *Dionysia* altogether uncanonical sexual paradigms were brought to public consciousness. After all, the soft, gentle Adonis was no more a master-rapist, ala Zeus or Heracles or Theseus, than were the maenads of Dionysus tame, harmless housewives. It is significant to note, as well, that the mysteries of Eleusis were open to all, men and women, slave and free alike.

Sharpening our focus now upon the theatre of Dionysus, it must be acknowledged that Euripides was not alone in voicing the complaints and in staging the conspiracies of women. In the years following the mutilation of the herms in the summer of 415 on the eve of the fateful Sicilian expedition, Aristophanes wrote several comedies - the *Lysistrata*,

119

the *Thesmophoriazousae,* and the *Parliament of Women* - on the theme
of women's rebellion. It has even been suggested that these plays were
inspired by a one-night women's revolt in 415 responsible for the
castration of herms throughout the city; and it must be admitted that this
account of the infamous scandal of the herms, whether true or false, has
an all but irresistible appeal. Sophocles too, despite his avowed
preference for depicting people as they ought to be, presented in his
lost *Tereus* [fr.524] the following quite frank assessment of the sorry lot
of contemporary women. Specifically, it is the voice of Procne, a
wronged wife if ever there was one, that we hear:

> ... So many times I have observed the status
>   of women, how we are nothing!
> While still girls in our father's house,
>   the life we enjoy is, I think,
>   the sweetest of all lives.
> Oblivion is a kind nurse,
>   the guarantor of childhood bliss.
> But when we ripen and come to our senses,
>   we are hurled from our houses.
> Far from our familar gods and our parents,
>   we are put on the market,
>   as objects for sale to men,
>   strangers or barbarians.
> Some of us go off to decent homes,
>   while others go off to abusive ones.
> Either way, after one agreeable night,
>   spent close in our husband's embrace,
>   we are expected to sing about our situation,
>   and to consider ourselves well-off.

Turning now to Euripides, we hear Procne's lament echoed in
the following speech of Medea, a similarly wronged and similarly vindictive
woman [*Medea,*230-251]:

> Of all creatures endowed with life-breath and wits,
>   we women form the sorriest lot.
> To begin with, it costs us a fortune

to buy our husbands;
and so we get a master for our bodies.
Our lot is still worse without one.
The greatest feat is to find a decent spouse,
instead of some worthless sort.
A woman has no respectable way out of a marriage;
neither can she say no to a man from the outset.
Every fresh wife finds herself in a house
whose ways and rules are new to her.
Without having learned such matters as a girl at home,
she would have to be psychic now
to know how best to make a life
with the man who shares a bed with her.
Now if she manages all of this to perfection;
and her husband lives with her gently,
placing on her neck a light yoke,
then hers is a life to be envied.
Otherwise, it is better to be dead.
A man, when he's had enough of his wife and family,
simply leaves the house,
finds a friend or a companion his own age,
and so puts an end to his boredome or disgust.
We women, however, must fix our eyes on a single soul,
forever.
What they tell us is that we women, living at home,
are spared the perils of war,
while they are out there nose to nose with spears.
What foolishness!
I'd three times rather take my chances
fighting in their front ranks,
than bear one of their children!

If there were fellow-women seated in the theatre of Dionysus, which remains an open question, these words must have found deep, though perhaps inaudible, resonance among them. In any event, they would have struck home somewhere. Medea is indeed *deine*, a woman to be reckoned with and wondered at. She is a strange woman; but, as her account of the common plight of women makes plain, there is nothing strange or remarkable in her situation. In short, Medea would have been

121

quite readily recognized. She is a woman whose mate has tired of her and has preferred to her a younger, more advantageously situated maiden, in this case no less than the king's daughter. Medea's mate is, of course, Jason, of Argonaut fame; and, like so many men who in the tradition cut a quite dashing mythic image, Jason suffers under the direct light of Euripides' critical realism. Like so many Greek icons, he is smashed on the Euripidean stage.

The truth of Jason, as it is disclosed in the *Medea*, is that he built his reputation on Medea's accomplishments. More than once he would have been a failure, even a dead man, if Medea had not bailed him out. For all of this she paid an exorbitant personal price, in return for which she seems to have expected no more than his lasting affection and loyalty. In short, she was willing to be the noteworthy woman behind the negligible man. But, in apparently timeless male, middle-aged fashion, Jason had ridden Medea like a horse for as long and far as her legs would carry him and then dismounted and looked around for a fresh mount to convey him to new heights. What else was a hero to do? As from gods, it would seem that Euripides came to expect little from heroes.

Jason's words, as it happens, are as reprehensible and recognizable as are his deeds. With altogether misdirected condescension, he claims and expects Medea to believe that this latest feat of his - his abandoning her and their two boys to marry the king's daughter - is a coup he has devised and accomplished with an unselfish eye to her, Medea's, well-being and that of their boys. His futile words, of course, fail to convince, as do most attempts in Euripidean drama to mask and remake deeds with words. Words, after all, are infinitely malleable and serve as readily to conceal as to reveal the truth. In both realms, in her words and in her deeds, Medea is more effective than her less than formidable male adversaries. She persuades them of her at least short-term goodwill and harmlessness; and, in the meantime, she destroys them.

Too much attention, I think, is paid by critics to the specifics of Medea's deeds and not enough to the specifics of her situation, which, unlike the extremity of her actions, link her to other women, then and since. In sketch, Medea is a woman without options, a woman against the wall. Having left a bloody trail behind her, she cannot retrace her steps in the hope of a happy homecoming. Without recourse to any bond of blood or marriage, she is, together with her sons, homeless. And, in ancient Greece, to be homeless is to possess no human niche at all.

Homeless, she and her children are mere prey, as good as dead, worse than dead. Even if Jason honors his word and makes some marginal provision for her safety and support, she is a woman shamed with nowhere to bury her rage and nothing worth waiting for but death. In sum, her situation is already atrocious before she envisions and enacts her atrocious response to it. Before Medea acts, she is cornered into a choice between two unacceptable possibilities. Either she can accept every abuse without reprisal until she is emptied of any pride or hope, or she can return abuse with abuse and regain her self-respect, if nothing else. It is clear from her encounter with Creon, that she has no access to human justice beyond that of her own revenge. Jason was prepared to leave Medea alive but with nothing to live for; and that is how she is prepared to, and does, leave him. Exiled from the house, she says that she will bring the whole house down, including her sons. Both Greek genetics and Greek politics place Jason's sons, whether he will have them or not, under his roof, as it were; and, when it comes down, it comes down on them too. The closest thing to a hapless bystander in the final carnage is Creon's daughter, who, if indeed she had any choice in the matter, betrayed the solidarity of women in accepting another woman's spouse as her own.

Medea's final solution is not true justice and is not presented or commended as such by Euripides. The fact remains, however, that poetic justice, however unacceptable it is in actuality, is imaginatively satisfying as civic justice rarely is. Revenge in kind, eye for eye, tooth for tooth, doing unto others as they had hoped to do to you, is as emotionally gratifying as it is ethically grotesque. Through the imaginative rehearsal of revenge within the marginally more safe precincts of the theatre, drama does, perhaps, as Aristotle later suggested, make possible the *catharsis* or purging of such extreme passions. At the very least, drama traces and thus explains their eruption into life, without condoning them. The clearest indication of how Euripides finally regards Medea is given by the fact that he stages her final appearance above the orchestra in the machine, the apparatus reserved for gods. She has, through her excessive, unrelenting savagery deified herself, as it were, won a place among the gods. Her final theophany reveals her acquired inhumanity, for this is the definitive characteristic of the Euripidean gods. Unlike the final redeeming moment of the *Hippolytus*, the final moment of the *Medea* is beyond the reach of forgiveness or compassion; for it is in the grip of a convert to the gods. And converts, as everyone knows, make up for lost time.

Another Euripidean woman against the wall was Hecuba. Like Medea, she had nothing left to lose in the end but her humanity; and, if we learn anything from Euripidean drama, we learn how tenacious our grip must be if our humanity is not to be ripped away from us. When her daughter Polyxena, who is everything to her, is dragged off so that the dead Achilles might drink her virgin blood splashed on his grave, Hecuba confesses that she is losing her grip; but that grip is not finally broken until she learns that her last hope has been betrayed by the family friend, Polymestor, pledged to protect the last surviving son of Priam and Hecuba. The boy's mutilated body washes ashore and is brought to Hecuba. The unthinkable is written in his wounds. Hecuba, like Medea, rootless now, tips into the inhuman torrent coursing through her and is carried off. Like Medea, she knows better than to expect divine justice and she soon exhausts every human appeal. Men, like the gods, are the authors of women's wretchedness; and they are not about to unwrite what they have written.

What is unique about Hecuba's revenge is that it represents the concerted revenge of a consortium of ravaged women. It is, in short, the work of collective female rage. In the *Medea*, the other women will no more join in Medea's reprisals than they will obstruct them. Their only complicity is their silence. In the *Bacchae*, the maenads are admittedly concerted in their savagery; but they do the work of the god and implement his rage, not their own. They are one with the god, possessed by him. Agave, so far from gloating in her bloody handiwork as does Hecuba, disbelieves it. In the *Hecuba*, we find the same utterly secular, psychlogically explicable female rage which is at work in the *Medea*, together with the collectivity of women emergent in the *Bacchae*.

This convergence represents an unanticipated and unsettling political development, as Agamemnon acknowledges as soon as he is apprised of it by Hecuba. When Hecuba says that, even without armed assistance from Agamemnon and his men, in fact with nothing more from him than his promise to obstruct any interference, she is prepared to deal with Polymestor and to see a bit of justice done, he is at once incredulous. He wonders how she can do this work alone; and, if not alone, with whose help. She reminds him of the *ochlos* [880], the mob, of Trojan women herded into nearby tents. He scoffs at her suggestion, presumably not because he sees mobs as harmless. After all, his mob

124

took Troy. "You mean **them**, the wild game we won with our spears?" [881] he taunts. Finally, when Agamemnon wonders how a mob of women is going to undo a king, Hecuba unveils a terrifying truth: "*deinon to plethos sun doloi te dusmachon.*" [884] It requires a good many more words to translate such distilled defiance. *Deine*, we recall, was Medea's epithet, a single word for what evokes at the same time dread and wonder. A familar definition of divine otherness as that which allures and terrifies, falls close to the mark here. Strange, fascinating, and fearful is the *plethos* of women. *Plethos* conveys both the sense of multiplicity and the sense of unity. In other words, Hecuba is saying something like this: just count the women in those tents and then imagine them acting as one. As if this were not enough to bring a shudder to the leader of men, Hecuba adds: *sun doloi te dusmachon*, which is to say, "put this together with cunning (in which we women have no peers) and there is no defence against us."

To all of this Agamemnon initially responds with one word, *deinon* [885], thus acknowledging Hecuba's assessment of the force within those tents. When he goes on to express his continuing doubts, Hecuba reminds him that there are precedents for their undertaking, citing the ninety-eight-percent effectiveness of the daughters of Danaus, and the women of Lemnos who outdid them. With this said, Hecuba has made her point; and so has Euripides. In a political order wherein the balance of power and weakness is the last word, the victimization of women is no law of nature. Rather, it is a function of women's isolation and passivity. If ever they should come to see their sufferings as one suffering and together trace it to its source, coming to a consciousness of their concerted power along the way, then the outcome will be indeed *deinon*, even blinding, a truth of which Polymestor soon becomes living proof.

Arrogantly unwary, Polymestor is easy prey to the cunning throng of women. After slashing the life from his sons, they fling Polymestor on his back, wrapping his hair in their hands and slammimg his head back against the rocky earth every time he tries to move. Straddling him like some netted beast, one by one the women plunge into the sockets of his eyes the pins taken from their loosened gowns until he streams with blood. The image is unmistakably sexual; the scenario one of gang-rape, an event all too familiar to these women and to their counterparts throughout the Athenian empire and points beyond.

125

At first glance, Hecuba may appear triumphant in all this. She destroys Polymestor utterly, with whatever satisfaction that brings. As in the *Medea*, however, the price of vengeance is ethically prohibitive. She pays with nothing less than her humanity for the pleasures of poetic justice. She and her fellow-women, as well as Polymestor, are utterly bestialized in the end, snarling and snapping at each other like dogs. In fact, lest there be any ambiguity regarding the ethical status of Hecuba, she is told that she will be literally transformed into a wild bitch with blazing eyes and will leap to her death from the mast of Agamemnon's ship before she ever reaches Greece. Thus, although the metaphysical destiny of Medea and of Hecuba stand at polar extremes from each other, they are equivalent in their inhumanity.

The truth which these reflections on the *Medea* and the *Hecuba* have laid bare is summed up by the chorus of the *Electra* [1051], when they point out that "justice can conduct itself shamefully." When we search both the *Medea* and the *Hecuba* for some ethical alternative to poetic justice, for someone who conducts herself without shame, our search inevitably comes to a rest with Polyxena and her sacrifice. Polyxena is, of course, only one of many young, unblemished sacrificial victims in Euripidean drama; but for now we will limit our considerations to her. As with Medea and with Hecuba, we must from the outset be clear regarding Polyxena's situation, her limits. She cannot choose whether to die or not. She knows that she is to have her throat slit this very day over the buried corpse of Achilles. True enough, there is a remote chance, to which her broken mother clings, of winning some reprieve or at least time from Odysseus, if she pleads pitifully with him; but she is aware that the only alternative to her announced sacrifice is a life of slavery, a living death the prospect of which is more dreadful to her than Neoptolemus' blade. Instinctively, and from watching her mother, she knows that suffering, up to a point, brings wisdom and challenges one to virtue, but that beyond a certain point suffering ravages and disfigures not only the body but often the soul as well. More specifically, she knows her own limits, knows that a girl like herself, accustomed to every comfort and unaccustomed to denial and degradation, will not bear with any grace the life of a slave. Her resolve is lucid and unflinching, as she addresses Odysseus with these words, words which we have already considered but which bear repetition here [*Hecuba*,342-368]:

126

Odysseus, I see you standing there at an angle,
    pulling back your hand into your cloak,
    fearful of being touched.
Don't be afraid.
I am not about to call upon Zeus,
    hope of the hopeless.
Nor am I going to beg for my life.
I have no choice but to die.
But as it happens, to die is my choice.
In resisting you, I would only die a shameful death,
    proving to be one of those who cling to life...
I was born a princess.
I was nursed on the highest of hopes,
    to be a bride for kings,
    vying for my hand.
I grew to be the acknowledged mistress
    of Troy's girls and women,
    conspicuous in every respect.
Mortality aside,
    I was a goddess.
And now I am a slave.
The name alone, so alien in every way,
    is enough to enamor me of death.
Am I to be an item for sale to coarse and brutal men,
    I, the sister of Hector,
    sister to the princes of Troy?
Am I to know only harsh necessity,
    sweeping some man's floors,
    kneading his bread,
    from one weary day to the next?
Am I, the bride of kings,
    to let some crude slave from god knows where
    defile me in his filthy bed?
Never!
I will take one last look at freedom
    and consign myself to hell.

Polyxena, led off to slaughter, maintains the same bravado before the voyeuristic veterans of Troy, drawn up in ranks to watch her sacrifice. As the son of Achilles approaches her with the whetted blade, he motions to his men to seize her, already bound. Polyxena, however, screams at them to stand off and for not one of them to touch her. At her bidding, they cut loose her hands. "I am the daughter of a king," she says. "I am not going down among the dead degraded as some man's slave." [551-552] Polyxena, her hands now free, takes her robe and tears it from her shoulder to below her waist, exposing her soft breasts. She leans back her neck in defiant acquiescence "to make it easy" for her executioner. Torn with pity, and perhaps with unacknowledged desire, Neoptolemus hesitates and then cuts her deep and clean below the chin, as her breath and blood burst from a single slit.

Polyxena is literally defeated; for her young life is effortlessly and irretrievably dispatched. In strength of arm, she is no match for one Greek warrior, much less for the whole Greek army. She does, however, manage to snatch from her literal undoing an human victory, an ethical victory, which, to eyes accustomed as Euripides' were to the darkness of the political realm, may be said to shine. After all, mortals are always literally defeated at the end of the day. The moral genius of mortality is to preserve one's integrity even as one is despoiled of all else, to die with grace even as one is damned.

It is clear that Hecuba and Polyxena represent two distinct, divergent possibilities for women in extremity, women at the mercy and disposal of men: the avenger and the martyr. In dramatic contrast with the avenger, the martyr remains spotless, uncontaminated by the violence she suffers. Witnessing her daughter's uncompromising purity of soul, Hecuba herself is moved. "There is beauty in your words, daughter," she says to Polyxena, "but it is a beauty wracked with pain." [382-383] Even as Hecuba wonders at the loveliness of leaving the world before it soils the soul, she finds that same loveliness lacking. She reveals complication, where Polyxena sees only simplicity; but beyond this Hecuba is not one to say more. Neither, it seems, is Euripides. In the *Hecuba*, he presents two unacceptable alternatives, which return today's reader and Euripides' own audience to the root of the dilemma, the corrupt political order in which women are often made to choose between degraded survival and innocent ruin. Hecuba, for her part, makes her choice; but, looking back at her daughter, Hecuba confesses herself to be nonetheless consoled by the exquisite nobility of the path taken by Polyxena.

At first glance, Iphigeneia, in her tragedy written by Euripides in self-imposed exile from Athens, might appear to be the mirror-image of Polyxena. Both Iphigeneia and Polyxena go to their deaths the would-be consorts of Achilles, the one in life and the other in death, the one before the war and the other after. Both supposedly die for the sake of fair winds, whether to waft the Greek armada on its way to Troy or to waft it home. Both take on their deaths freely with the same piquant defiance of brute force. What separates them, however, is the fact that, while Polyxena dies in lucid despair, Iphigeneia dies in the thrall of a glorious delusion.

The truth soon disclosed in the *Iphigeneia in Aulis* is that Agamemnon's ambition has outstripped his abilities. He is no more in control of his army than was Hippolytus in control of his horses. The army has its own reasons for setting out to Troy and they have nothing to do with retrieving Helen nor with restoring Greek pride. The army's lust, its driving compulsion, is for violence and for gold. What is more, Calchas, the war-mongering cleric, has convinced the army that Iphigeneia's death is a divine demand. Hers must be the first blood spilt. Only then can the army slake its own thirst with Troy. The dark truth is that Agamemnon is so enamored of his prerogatives, so enslaved by his fears, that he is willing to kill his own beloved girl rather than compromise his career or confront the truth. And not only does he dispatch his daughter to death; but he sends her off into legend bearing a seductively glistening lie, whose perversity she is too young and too desperate to detect. In other words, he takes advantage not only of her weakness but also of her innocence. He spoils her even as he slays her.

We shed unwarranted light on this darkest of tragedies if we imagine that Agamemnon believes a word of what he tells Iphigeneia regarding why she must die. In utterly lucid bad faith, Agamemnon creates a lie the size of the atrocity he is willing and about to commit. He invents Hellas, Greece, an entity greater than the sum of all of its living daughters and sons; and so it must be if it is to demand and to justify their deaths, as many of them as are needed. He invents too the barbarians, not in their flesh but as a provocative political fantasy, barbarians whose very existence is an affront and a threat, and whose extinction or subjection thus becomes a moral imperative. In short, Agamemnon re-invents, before our eyes, politics. He subverts the simple love of life and of all that sustains it into patriotism, the sentimental love of an ideal, fictive historical entity, in this case Greece, which masks, while pretending to transcend, the shabby self-interest of moral non-entities like Agamemnon and Menelaus and the mob which flatters itself as an army, a national assault-force, marshalled to make Greek beds safe investments again.

What darkens and complicates this tragedy is that Iphigeneia is being murdered by her own father, not by some savage stranger. Neither Agamemnon nor Iphigeneia can confront this truth straight on. They share, instead, a consoling lie. Agamemnon plants its seed in Iphigeneia and she brings it to term. Greece is turning to him and to her and demanding the ultimate sacrifice. Nothing less than the freedom of Greece is at stake. With this lie, Agamemnon anaesthetizes his girl before putting her under the knife. But we should not mistake this act for one of compassion. Anaesthesia can be as much for the surgeon's convenience as for the patient's comfort; and in this instance Agamemnon's prevailing concern is to ease his own passage to Troy, not his daughter's passage to Hades. Her death is something he wants to put behind him with as little awkwardness and delay as possible. Like every sacrifical victim, Iphigeneia must show herself willing. With a handful of grain or a cup of water, cattle were made to nod their heads and goats to shiver in assent to the blade. In the case of a human victim, especially one's own daughter, the stratagem must be more subtle and perverse. Agamemnon is, of course, prepared to admit none of this. Instead, he cries out in futile contradiction of the obvious: "I love my children! If I did not, I would be deranged." [1256] "Woman," Agamemnon says to Clytemnestra, "it is a strange and dreadful thing [*deinon*] to be daring to do what I am about to do." [1257] Given that he regards the alternative to be equally dreadful, however, he goes ahead and does it anyway.

Clytemnestra reminds Agamemnon that Iphigeneia will not be the first of her children torn from her arms and slain by his hand. She was first taken to Agamemnon's bed by force, after he had murdered her husband Tantalus and shattered her new-born infant's skull against the hard earth. This bit of family history serves to put the immediate course of events in perspective. The present atrocity is not some rare cosmic eclipse of an otherwise exceptionless regard for the sacredness of life. Instead, it is the most recent incident in a recurrent pattern of atrocities. It is the fruit of war, the first-fruit of a new harvest. Tell me, Clytemnestra taunts her husband [1185-1190]:

130

After you've sacrificed your girl,
  what are your prayers going to sound like?
What sort of blessing does a child-slaughterer like you
  ask for?
When you go off leaving a trail of shame,
  will you not come home reeking?
And how is it any more fitting for me
  to beg the gods to bless you?
Wouldn't we as much as call the gods idiots,
  if we were to ask blessings,
  for those who murder our children?

What Agamemnon receives from Clytemnestra is no blessing but a threat. She will be waiting for him.

Meanwhile, Iphigeneia, her frenzied fear of death now sublimated into her new-found sense of mission, explains to her mother that "It is wrong for me to love life too much. You bore me, not only for yourself but as the common property of all of Greece." [1385-1386] She regards herself now no longer pitiable but privileged. She is to be the bride of Greece; the bright events of Troy will be her progeny. The irony lost on her is that she, a corpse, will breed only other corpses, Polyxena among them. The bright events of Troy will be no brighter than the one about to occur. All the same, Iphigeneia is committed now to playing out to its perverse consummation the charade of a marriage with which this tragedy began. She insists that there be no mourning, no funeral mound, no laments. "Shout the paean," [1467-1468] she cries out to her attendants, only highlighting the dark ambiguity of the moment; for paeans were sung not only before wedding banquets but also before battles.

The poetic and ritual parallels between sacrifice and marriage embedded in this play are too many and too rich in implication to trace fully here. In outline, however, they are unmistakable. The original lie which lured Iphigeneia to Aulis took the form of a summons to marriage; and the final lie which lures Iphigeneia to her death takes a similar form. Such a ploy is uniquely suited to possess the imagination of an adolescent princess. Between Iphigeneia and her wedding, however, there stands a ritual requirement, the *proteleia*, the preliminary sacrifice. Agamemnon and Clytemnestra and Iphigeneia share the same impatience to put the *proteleia* behind them and to get on with the main event. The main event is, however, a war not a wedding. Iphigeneia will not soon lie under her husband and spill her first blood in the act of love. Instead, in an act more hideous than incest, she will lie under her own father and spill her first blood as he plunges his blade into her virgin heart. She will die "like a spotless young animal." [1083] Instead of a love-cry, there will be only the scream of death.

For many critics, the radical conversion of Iphigeneia to her fate is too sudden and too complete to be believed. While it may be admitted that events, inward or outward, seldom take as long on a Greek stage as they do in everyday experience, we must appreciate that Iphigeneia has very little time at her disposal. As for the seamlessness of her resolve, what less would sustain her now? Besides, it only has to last another hour. If we are surprised to find no single crack in her new-found faith, we need only to recall that the truth masked by it is so hideous that, like the face of Medusa, one glimpse of it would turn Iphigeneia to stone. Like Perseus, the most that she can bear is a reflection of the monster only a blade's length away, however distorted that image may be; and there is no one who can begrudge her that. If her words sound hollow, it is because they most surely are. They are the words of speeches, sheer propaganda, designed to put down the soul like a dog that has outlived its purpose.

The *Iphigeneia in Aulis* is Euripides' last word on war, the politics which provoke it, and the victims who endure it. Surely we do not learn from this play but are nevertheless reminded by it that no war, not even the Trojan War, and much less the Peloponnesian War, would ever or long be fought without seducing the young to its awful momentum. Young, beautiful bodies and souls must be given some compelling reason for dying or for killing; and those whose purposes are served by war know well that the truth will not do. It is cursedly the case that the inexperience, idealism, passion, and naivete of youth conspire to make them prey to the speeches of their elders. The timeless scandal is that the latter, like Agamemnon, cynically aware of the power of their words and their effect, believe not a single word they say. "A smooth tongue," indeed, "is a mischievous and malignant thing." [333]

Set ineffectually against the practitioners and apologists of violence are those who most often endure it, women first among them. The mark of womanhood in ancient Greece was motherhood and "motherhood is a strange, powerful thing [*deinon*], a great love-charm, giving this much in common to all women: there is nothing they will not

132

do or endure for their children." [917-918] Women's biological destiny is to give life; and it may be that they find it that much more difficult to squander it. It may be too that their traditionally assigned place of weakness in the political order gives them a peculiarly privileged vantage-point on the madness of male militarism. There seems to be little question in Euripidean drama that power corrupts and that absolute power corrupts absolutely. Thus women, by dint of their very weakness, are likely to be more humanly intact. Yet, as we have seen, weakness pushed to the brink, suffering beyond the point of endurance, can be every bit as corrupting as power. No wonder, then, that Euripides often turns to women not yet dispossessed of their instincts to speak the simplest, most telling truths. "To look upon the light of day," says Iphigeneia before she succombs to fear and to her father's spell [1250-1252],

> is for all human beings the sweetest of joys.
> In the dark world below, there is nothing.
> To pray for death is sheer madness.
> To be alive, in whatever lowly condition,
>   is better than to die a glorious death.

Of course, Iphigeneia herself soon betrays her own words; but their truth stands and reveals itself to those under less immediate duress than she.
    These straight, simple words and others like them in the Euripidean corpus call into radical question the traditional heroic code rooted in *philotimia*, the questing desire to be always more than the others, to increase as they decrease. To enter the *agōn*, the contest, one must step into the ring of death, willing to despoil or to be despoiled, to kill or to die.
Outside that ring there is no glory, only life. Inside that ring, however, if Euripides' voice has any validity and resonance left at all, is only madness. It is a ring of fools.

> Ten thousand men
>   dream ten thousand different dreams.
> Some of them come true and end in bliss.
> Nothing at all comes of the rest.
> What I call blessed is the life lived in simple happiness,
>   day by day. [*Bacchae*, 907-909]

133

The life exorcised of *philotimia*, or never first infected by it, is best. For one thing, such a life is harmless. Larger than life dreams are, in themselves, life-threatening. To avoid all suffering, either the inflicting of it or the enduring of it, is admittedly a dream larger or better than life, an ideal rarely if ever to be achieved; but the pursuit of it will, at worst, do no harm. "No more is to be hoped for by anyone in any life," says Hecuba, "than to elude ruin, one day at a time." [*Hecuba*,627-628]

It is a simple doctrine, if it may be called that, which comes through in these and countless other moments in Euripidean drama. Here is a code of heroism scaled to the human, accomodated to the darkness of the political order. In succinct formulation, the Euripidean hero is the survivor. Archaic heroism, by contrast, excluded from the outset all those who clung to life. Survival was worthy of women and cowards. In the new heroism of Euripides, however, survival is the essential human virtue; and at the core of this survival is the blind and uncompromising affirmation of life, the affirmation pulsing in nature, in *hygra phusis*, the affirmation annually enacted in the resurrection of the world from the dark death of winter and celebrated in the rites of Dionysus and Demeter, the affirmation mortally imitated and shared in the act of childbirth. Nowhere in Euripidean drama is this blind, wild, and wondrous bond between mother and child, with all of its cosmic resonances, more lyrically recited than in the *Helen* [1319-1352], wherein the chorus sing of the delirium of the Great Mother when her child is abducted into the darkness below the earth:

> The sorrowing mother searched far and wide
> For any clue to her daughter's rape,
> A crime accomplished with effortless guile.
> But at last she called an end to her toil,
> Whose only fruit was frenzy and exhaustion.
> Then to the snow-white crest of Ida she climbed,
> Wherein mountain nymphs keep constant watch.
> There the mother broken with grief
> Cast herself down among the rocky thickets
>   blanketed in snow.
> So she brought blight upon the barren earth,
> Making the snow sterile, unyielding of any fruit.
> Total was the ruin she brought to the race of men.
> For the sheep and the cattle she provided nothing,

No fresh, leafy fodder, no curling green tendrils.
Cities lost their means of life.
The gods went without their offerings.
The altar flames went out.
And with a mother's endless grief,
Bitter for her daughter lost and gone,
She sealed shut the earth's springs.
The glistening streams went dry.

When the raving mother brought to a halt
Even the festivals shared by gods and men,
It was Zeus who gave the kind command
To calm the woman's hellish rage.
"Go, sacred graces, Muses too, go to Deio,
Crazed for the girl that is gone.
With wild cries pierce her dark resolve.
With dance and sweet song soften her heart's pain."
First to respond was Aphrodite,
Loveliest of all the blessed ones,
Who took in her hand the skin-taut tambourine,
Rimmed with brazen castanets.
And soon her clamor reached the depths of hell,
Where a smile broke across the goddess-mother's face,
As she took up the blaring flute,
And in the wildness of it all,
Rediscovered joy.

If we forget, as we do and must, that this is a myth about gods, it
tells a familiar tale of the frenzied love of mother for child, the desolation
of irretrievable loss, and the miraculous rebirth of the human spirit
insatiate with life. The pure, unqualified affirmation of life, emerging as it
often does from beneath the heaviest burdens and within the darkest
griefs is the core of human courage and grandeur.

Concerning the altogether uncanonical heroism of survival
exhibited in Euripidean drama, certain possible misconceptions require
to be addressed. Firstly, by "survival" is meant more than the mere
sustenance of life-signs. The only survival worthy of a Euripidean hero is
human survival, the integral survival of soul as well as body. To save
one's skin, as it were, while abandoning one's integrity, is not something

135

admired in Euripidean drama. It would be difficult to argue, for instance, that the characters of Electra, Orestes, and Pylades, as they are drawn in the *Orestes*, are respected, much less celebrated, by the playwright. Although, or perhaps because, they will stop at nothing to preserve their lives, they are portrayed as nothing less than psychopathic terrorists. The fact that Apollo distributes rewards to these three at the close of the play is damning, not redeeming. What Apollo furnishes is an Olympian "political" solution, whose ludicrous contradiction of common sense and of common decency is nowhere more evident than in his proclamation that Orestes is to marry the same girl against whose throat he is at that very moment pressing his blade. Apollo's solution is virtually transparent to the numerous treaties already negotiated by "Olympian" Athens with an unswerving eye to its own survival and self-interest and blind to all else. It may even anticipate the inevitable terms which Athens would soon be forced to negotiate with Sparta; for the allusions to Athens in the *Orestes* are woven of the sheerest fabric. "There is not much to be done with a fallen house," [70] laments Electra, summing up her woes in the prologue. Like the house of Agamemnon, Athens in 408 was imminently threatened from without and rotting from within, leaving everyday doubts whether it would first be torn down or cave in. Orestes, Electra, Orestes, Pylades, and Athens were all indisputably "survivors"; but we find little pity or esteem displayed in the *Orestes* for their brand of survival

Secondly, if survival is to be appropriately human, it must be not only integral but communal. The Euripidean ethic of survival is not a code of selfishness, preoccupied with personal longevity and purity. Euripidean survival is inseparable from solidarity; and nowhere do we find this solidarity more frequently and fully displayed than among women. Euripidean drama is rife with references to the actual and active fellowship of women. In the *Helen* [329], for instance, the chorus, endeavoring to convince Helen that she is not alone but companioned in her trials, explains that "it is only right for one woman to bear another's burdens." Similarly, in the *Iphigeneia in Tauris* [1061], Iphigeneia invokes the natural consortium of women, prefacing her appeal for loyalty with the following words: "We are all women and the good-will we bear each other runs in our blood."

Women's communal affirmation of life, however, is not restricted, in principle, to the *genos* or race of women but extends appropriately to the race of mortals, as well. If Euripidean women are, in practice, somewhat exclusive in their political concerns, it is because they are so

136

often herded into tents as slaves or confined to their quarters as wives. It is they who are excluded from public affairs; and it would be one more undeserved affront to make them answer for their separateness. Indeed, it is not surprising that we possess few historical or literary accounts of women's engagement in the wider community, beyond the community of women and of their children. One such account, however, may be found in the *Phoenician Women*, wherein it is the women, young and old, Greek and barbarian, royalty and slaves, who display enlightened and unselfish concern for the common good, while their male counterparts would gladly destroy the city and each other before relinquishing their petty quarrels and private ambitions.

Once again, in the *Phoenician Women*, an ancient myth is held by Euripides at such an angle as to mirror events of his own city and of his own time. Thebes seems only a mask worn by Athens in this play. The chorus' description of Thebes [250-252] - "a city wrapped in a dense cloud of spears, the air ablaze with the spectre of an impending battle and its carnage" - might as well describe Athens in any of the years from 411 to 408, when this play was likely written and performed. Athens too, like Thebes, was in tatters by this time, worn thin by war and shredded by factionalism. Both stood on the brink of doom. Within this apocalyptic context, the strong, public, challenging voice of Jocasta is particularly engaging. She is a rare Greek woman, on active duty in the front ranks of political negotiation, denouncing squarely every warring faction, and pleading with fierce will and wit the cause of equality and peace; and all this while her husband, blind and despairing, lies behind bolted doors. We may wonder whether Jocasta's royalty, her near-widow status, and perhaps her arrival at menopause suffice to account for her freedom to engage in public affairs. We might indeed speculate that in the figure of Jocasta we are permitted a glimpse of a phenomenon occuring in Athens in the late fifth-century. As the Peloponnesian War dragged on, year by year thinning out the able male population of Athens, and particularly after the staggering loss of Athenian lives in Sicily, the ratio of mature women to men must have been decisively altered, leaving women not only with numerical superiority, but with correspondingly expanded freedoms and even responsibilities. Such has been the rule during other, even less protracted wars in history, such as the two global wars of this century; and such, we might surmise, was the case in Athens. Confronted with history's nearly unbroken silence on this matter, we cannot say more with any confidence.

137

Euripides, of course, could not rewrite the history of Athens, any more than Jocasta could turn back the torrent of events in Thebes. She was ineffectual; and her counterparts in Athens, if indeed she had any, were not only ineffectual but fell from whatever slight influence they may have held without a trace. What remains significant, however, is that in re-telling a story as transparently allegorical as this one was for the citizens of Athens, Euripides raised Jocasta from traditional political irrelevance and not only assigned to her a central public role but also gave to her a voice that was lucid, articulate, and visionary. Clearly she is the only person in Thebes, as re-enacted in the *Phoenician Women*, who emerges as a possible savior of the city. As potential rulers of Thebes, Eteocles, Polyneices, and Creon, in other words all of the viable male candidates, are blind in one way or the other to the common good and disinclined to its pursuit. If the citizens of Athens were left with a similar response to the *Phoenician Women* and if their imaginations leapt to their own city under siege, bled nearly white, and still hemorrhaging from within, did the words of contemporary women, known to them but lost to us, come to mind, words like those of Jocasta, pleading for an end to savagery and for an embracing of peace, simplicity of life, and equality? Perhaps they were as blind as the sons of Oedipus, in which case the chorus' words were likely addressed to them: "the city, if it could chance upon it senses, would weep." [1344]

The spectre of *gynecocracy*, women's power or women's rule, was clearly, if we consult a wide range of traditional and fifth-century sources, an object of profound suspicion and fear. Together with rampant promiscuity and bizarre mating practices, permissiveness towards women, much less submission to them, came to be associated with barbarians, and to some lesser extent with Spartans. The prospect of power's coming into the hands of women through peaceful and proper means was all but unimaginable. In the Athenian male imagination, women, if they were ever to come to power, would do so in the same manner as would slaves, through their seizing power suddenly and violently, slaughtering their husbands or their masters indiscriminately. Even the influence of women was something pronouncedly suspect and to be avoided. Women, in sum, like barbarians and slaves, were thought to be intellectually inferior, unruly, devious, sexually uninhibited, potentially dangerous, and representative, over all, of a lower form of life. Although Euripides occasionally employed these stereotypes for reasons of his own, he also boldly contradicted them in too many

138

instances to catalogue here, displaying at least their irrelevance to, and often their reversal of, the truth. One example might suffice.

In the *Trojan Women*, Andromache describes how she, or any captive woman, evokes the instant hate of her new master and mate, if she loyally lingers at all in memories of her slaughtered spouse. Instead, she is expected to spread wide not only her legs but even her heart to this savage stranger; and accompanying such abuse there is expressed the following theory about women and sex, to which Andromache makes her own seething response [665-672]:

> What they say is
>> that all any man has to do
>> to make a woman lose her aversion for his bed
>> is to show her a good time for one night.
>
> I would spit from my sight
>> that woman who would throw off the man
>> whose bed she used to share,
>> and resume the ways of love with another.
>
> Even a young filly, torn from her running-mate,
>> balks at being yoked with another.
>
> Yet it is a dumb brute beast,
>> born without wits
>> and without a glimmer of our nature.

In this light, it is not women who are found to display a lower life-form, evidenced in savage sexuality.

Fear, hate, and violence go hand in hand; and women in Athens were the privileged object of all three. In the prism of Euripidean drama, however, all three are refracted back upon their source. Nowhere is this fact more manifest than in Euripides' treatment of the figure of Helen, surely the most hated of all Greek women, Helen the whore, Helen the ruin of cities. However relatively benign Homer's treatment of Helen had been, her name had made the rounds by the fifth century. Indeed, she emerged as the sum of all that is both irresistibly alluring and deservedly despised in women, the virtual embodiment of Hesiod's *kalon kakon*.

An adequate tracing of the image of Helen in fifth-century tragedy, or even in the Euripidean corpus, would require extensive citing and analysis of sources. A more brief and bold sketch, however, is called for to conclude this section on women; and I trust that the following few

139

comments would hold up under closer, more inclusive scrutiny. Setting aside the *Helen* for a moment, essentially two possible accounts of Helen's misadventure to Troy are circulated in Euripides' plays. She may have gone to Troy quite willingly, in the thrall of a freshly excited lust; or she may have been torn violently from her home and her husband and made a captive lover in Troy. In weighing these two versions and ferreting out the more likely truth of the matter, at least as Euripides saw it, the *Trojan Women* would appear to be a privileged source; for therein the trial of Helen is effectively enacted, and the principal surviving witnesses made to take the stand. The testimony of Cassandra, given her powers, is enough to convict; but Helen damns herself by admitting that she ran away on her own feet, yet, she claims, as a slave, not to Paris but to Aphrodite, the irresistible. Helen rests her case on what she imagines to be theological bedrock; but in the Euripidean theatre her rock softens to sand. What Hecuba says is what everyone here knows: "Aphrodite is merely a name for mortal lust." [989] And with this said, Helen has no case left. The Euripidean verdict is evident. Helen left Menelaos freely; for she loved Paris more.

Helen is accused of a good deal more, however, than adultery. At her door are laid all of the agonies of Troy, every corpse and every maimed life, Trojan or Greek, left in the wake of a ten-year war; and, strangely enough, it is Hecuba who unwittingly speaks in defense of Helen with respect to this latter, more grievous and sweeping charge. No one here hates Helen more than does Hecuba; and no one is more uncompromising in her demands that Helen must be made to suffer all that she has coming to her. Nonetheless, it is Hecuba, who, after cataloguing her disasters, those endured already and those yet to be endured, points out a curious fact. "And all this," she says, "what has been and what will be, happened because of one woman's love affair." [498-499]

What Hecuba notices is that all Helen actually did was to take a lover. She fell in love. She did not wage a war. The war was not her idea or her doing. The war was not the effect of what Helen did but rather Menelaus' and Agamemnon's response to what Helen did. Just as she chose love freely, they chose war freely; and, in doing so, they revealed their characters, characters utterly exposed in others of Euripides' plays. The simple fact is that Helen and Paris represented another path from the one worn by the Greek warlords. After all, Paris had been offered both lordship and conquest, either one of which would have pinned

140

Agamemnon and Menelaus under his heel; but he chose beauty and love instead. Helen and Paris both preferred love to all else and thus preferred each other to anyone else. The war and all its carnage and rubble was someone else's preference, someone else's choice.

Why, then, war? Euripides' most concise answer to this comes in the *Helen*. His answer is: for nothing, always for nothing. In this same play he exonerates Helen utterly. Drawing upon a variant tradition regarding her, he explains that she never went to Troy at all. Not only is she innocent of causing the war; but she is innocent even of adultery. The Greek armies pursued and fought over a fantasy, a puff of air, nothing more. Euripides, writing this play as the first survivors staggered home from Sicily with stories of a defeat beyond belief, must have decided that it was time for the truth to come home to roost.

Helen was the consummate Greek woman; and Euripides leaves her utterly untarnished. In the last speech of the *Helen* [1686-1687], Theoclymenus, the failed Egyptian Paris, to whose unrelenting advances the faithful Helen never once succumbed, has this to say about the once most hated of women:

> In the name of Helen, the noblest of spirits,
>   and for that reason an exceptional woman,
>   I bless you all.

In the *Helen*, Euripides returns Helen to Argos to clear her own name; and, with the same play, he returns women to Athens with the same prospect in sight. Women, no matter what Hesiod wrote and Greek men believed, are not the cause of the world's woes. We need look elsewhere. These words from the *Melanippe* [fr.499.1-3] likely overstate Euripides' own estimation of women; but they are miles closer to the truth than the charge of misogyny lodged against him all these years. Anyway, if justice, while in process, is a matter of balance, the citing of them might serve its cause

> The censure and abuse women suffer
>   from the tongues of men
>   are sheer madness.
> They are bending an empty bow.
> The truth is that women are better than men,
>   a truth I will disclose.

Finally, we must note that, in saying that women are better than men, the word chosen by Euripides for man is not *aner* whose opposite is *gune*, man as opposed to woman or husband as opposed to wife, but rather is *arsen* whose opposite is *thelus*, muscular, aggressive man as opposed to tender, nourishing woman. What this fact may suggest is that women are not being categorically compared and preferred to men, but rather that women's characteristic way of being in the world, of inhabiting their humanity, which is presumably available to men for imitation, is what outshines and shames the ethically homuncular machismo characteristic of men.

SLAVES AND BARBARIANS

This discussion of the political order has so far been focused on women precisely because women dominate the Euripidean corpus. If we consider only Euripides' seventeen extent dramas, we find that eight of these bear the names of women, while twelve may be said to be primarily about women; and fourteen have choruses composed of women. Apart from these statistical indications of the thematic prominence of women in Euripidean drama, it may be argued that the condition of women as explored in Euripides' plays epitomizes the corruption of the political order as he understood it. In contrast with his evident preoccupation with women and their issues, Euripides makes only occasional mention of slaves and barbarians. Consequently, the following comments will constitute little more than a series of footnotes to our discussion of women.

The issues of slavery and racism are all but inseparable from those of sexism. In all three, violence and oppression are rooted in prejudice. Women, slaves, and barbarians are defined by *nomos*, law and custom, as "other" than, and correspondingly unequal to, free, male, Athenian citizens; and, since, within the city, citizenship is functionally equivalent with humanity, otherness is functionally equivalent with inhumanity. Women, slaves, and barbarians are all three races apart and thus the object of systematic misunderstanding and institutional violence. We may speculate why Euripides chose to highlight the

142

misunderstanding and violence endured by women. Not only by virtue of their numbers, but even more by virtue of their inevitable proximity to men - as their mothers, sisters, daughters, wives, and lovers - women were unavoidable. This proximity may have made it all the more difficult for men, including Euripides, to insulate themselves from the feelings and views of women and to exclude them from the human circle. The otherness of barbarians and slaves was likely easier, conceptually and emotionally, to maintain.

The issues of women, slaves, and barbarians are inseparable, as well, because these three categories overlap regularly on the Athenian stage, as they did in Athenian homes and streets. Most slaves were either women or barbarians or both. Even Athenian wives bore their own resemblances to slaves. Whether taken in war or taken in marriage, women were always vulnerable to a form of slavery. Curiously and tellingly, brides as well as newly acquired slaves, were welcomed into their new homes with the *katachysmata*, the ritual pouring of nuts down upon their heads. Both wives and slaves were regarded as property; and whatever marginal status they possessed under the law was derived from that fact. Wives and slaves were not only at the service of their husbands and masters but also at their disposal sexually. The lot of slaves, however, was undeniably heavier and darker than that of Athenian wives, particularly those slaves consigned to the mines and quarries, for which hell is a euphemism. Whatever reputation fifth-century Athenians may enjoy to this day for having been gentle masters, the evidence to the contrary, such as the common practice of torturing slaves publicly in the state-operated interrogation center, remains, as it always has been, damning. Slavery is not a gentle institution, however administered; and there is little to suggest that the Athenians administered it mildly.

So far from appearing an unnatural atrocity, slavery seems to have been regarded by Athenians in the fifth century as an integral element of advanced civilization, at least so long as slavery was limited to barbarians. A great many Greeks seem to have had qualms about enslaving other Greeks, which is to say that slave-holding was mostly justified in Athens as it was in America by the presumption of racial superiority. Theories to this effect were expounded, for instance, in the fifth-century Hippocratic treatise, *Air, Waters, Places,* and later, in the fourth century, by Aristotle. The above Hippocratic treatise traces the peculiar convergence of intelligence and courage characteristic of Greeks to their geographical location and its accompanying climatic

143

influences. In the *Politics*, clearly drawing upon this and other sources, Aristotle restates the case for Greek racial superiority and points out that, provided they achieve political unity, the race of Greeks constitutes a natural master-race. This claim, however, must have been a by-word already in the fifth-century, as well; for we find it shamelessly proclaimed by the hapless Iphigeneia, at Aulis. "It seems like common sense, mother," she says to Clytemnestra, "that Greeks should rule over barbarians, and not barbarians over Greeks." [1400-1401] In this too, however, she is deluded by her father, a delusion we cannot imagine to have been shared by Euripides when we consider the very next line spoken by Iphigeneia in defense of the claim for the seemingly natural rule of Greeks over barbarians.: "For they are slaves and we are free." [1401] The patent ludicrousness of Iphigeneia's perception that she and her mother, and for that matter her father, are free, makes this one of Euripides' most bitterly ironic lines, an irony which surely reflects back one line upon what seems to Iphigeneia and, presumably, to "Greece" to be common sense.

In the *Politics*, Aristotle makes a general reference to those who argue that slavery is contrary to nature and is a construct of law or convention. From this reference it is clear that the case against slavery was well-known by the last third of the fourth century, although the only direct statement of this case prior to Aristotle comes, compliments of a scholiast to the *Rhetoric* [1273b], from Gorgias' pupil, Alcidamas, who claimed that "God has set all men free. Nature has made no one a slave." Similarly, regarding the natural equality of all races, the fourth-century liberal, Antiphon, argued that in all things nature has constituted Greek and barbarian alike. In all the essentials of humanity, Greek and barbarian, he claimed, are identically endowed.

In the fifth century, however, Euripides comes the closest of anyone to arguing for the essential equality of all human beings, men and women, masters and slaves, Greeks and barbarians. Both because as a playwright he necessarily speaks with many voices and because he chose to speak more obliquely than later prose-writing liberals, it is not possible to point to or even to reconstruct a straight-forward, Euripidean refutation of racism and slavery. Indeed, it is possible to catalogue a rather loathesome list of statements by Euripidean characters who have little good to say of slaves and nothing bad to say of slavery. One such statement comes from the *Alexandros* [fr.49]: "So worthless is the race of slaves! All belly, they never look beyond (their next meal)." In such instances, however, if we look to the immediate sources of such comments, to the characters who utter them, we find that they are mostly unsympathetic, even contemptible. Once again, as in the case of misogyny, we must note not only what is spoken, but by whom, in what context, and, most elusive of all, in what likely tone it is spoken. In short, we must confront the fact once again that Euripides wrote plays and not essays.

We have already indicated within Euripides' plays various speeches expressing the general disavowal of any natural distinctions between human beings, which implies a disavowal of the essential superiority or inferiority of any sub-category of human beings such as men, women, nobility, peasants, bastards, slaves, Greeks, and barbarians. We have also seen how, at the same time, the very structure of Euripidean drama is transparent to a spectrum of power and weakness descriptive of the oppression inflicted by some human beings on others. In other words, however untruthful it may be to the essential equality of all human beings and to the harmony which ought to proceed from that equality, it is nonetheless a truth, in the sense of a political fact, that divisions, however unnatural, are asserted and enforced by certain human individuals and groups over against other human individuals and groups. Finally, the dramatic acknowledgement of both truths - the metaphysical truth of human equality and the political fact of inequality - necessarily creates an ambiguity in the voice of Euripides, which requires interpretations whose legitimacy cannot be proven.

With respect to Euripides' own specific questions and commitments regarding slavery and racism, I would only hint here at such an interpretation. Neither the sources within Euripides' plays nor the space remaining within this chapter give warrant to anything beyond a few brief concluding remarks here. First, with respect to slavery, Euripides frequently dissolves the concept, pointing out that even the most privileged and powerful men, standing at what seem to be the furthest human remove from slavery, men such as Agamemnon in the *Hecuba* and in the *Iphigeneia in Aulis*, are best described as slaves. Thus, in the *Hecuba* [864-869], when Agamemnon explains to Hecuba the constraints upon him, she concludes:

> Then there is no such thing as a free mortal.
> All are slaves of money or of fate.
> Whether for fear of standing out against the crowd,

or of breaking the city's laws,
each one is bent into compliance,
against all his better instincts.
I see your terror,
how you defer to the mob;
so allow me to set you free from your fear.

Hecuba, a woman and a slave, in an ironic reversal of roles, proposes to calm the fears of the king of kings; and, as if to confirm the truth of this reversal, the same Agamemnon, in the opening episode of the *Iphigeneia in Aulis*, is found envying his own servant-slave. Euripides further dissolves the concept of slavery by frequently giving noble natures to his slaves and base natures to his nobles. Under such a critique, slavery is denied any basis whatsoever in racial superiority or indeed in any superiority other than that of power. Repeatedly, Euripidean characters assert with their words and confirm with their actions that slavery resides solely in the name, the designation, of slave, assigned arbitrarily and kept in place by blind force. "The shame borne by slaves," we hear in the *Ion* [854-856], "resides solely in their name. In every other way, slaves, provided they lead decent lives, are the equals of the free."

The same arguments may be and are made on behalf of barbarians. Although Euripides not only presents anti-barbarian prejudice in action but may also be himself accused of presenting what may be called "stage-barbarian" characters, such as Theoclymenus in the *Helen*, Thoas in the *Iphigeneia in Tauris*, and the Phrygian slave in the *Orestes*, the overall effect of his treatment of barbarians is to dissolve the category of barbarian in much the same fashion as he did that of slave. Greeks regularly prove themselves more barbarous than non-Greeks, who in turn prove themselves on occasion quite endearing and benign. Theoclymenus and Thoas, to cite two notable barbarians, for all their fuming witlessness, are finally less savage than their Greek counterparts. Their childish superstitions and incapacity for cunning leave them at the mercy of Greeks to whom deception and calculation are second nature. In short, behind the buffoonery of these and certain other Euripidean barbarians, we may discern a disarming innocence and simplicity long lost by more cynical, sophisticated Greeks. Barbarians, like slaves and women, are quite commonly the victims of Greek violence, a violence strategically justified by their racial and moral inferiority. "That's barbarians

146

for you," rants Hermione, who has no recognizable virtues of her own to flaunt, "they're all the same - father and daughter, mother and son, brother and sister, all doing it with each other, murdering their way out of family quarrels - law means nothing to them." [*Andromache*,173-176] Speaking as one barbarian who suffers immeasurably from the violence unleashed and rationalized by Greek prejudice, Andromache, in the *Trojan Women* [764], minces no words: "You Greeks invented barbarian perversions."

The archetypal barbarians in Euripidean drama are, it would seem, the Trojans, just as the Trojan War is the archetypal war. It is instructive in this light to reflect upon Cassandra's assessment of Greek and Trojan losses in that war. In sum, the Greeks lost not only their lives but their souls. In her eyes, which see all, Troy, though in ashes, is blessed beside Greece; for, while the Greeks won shame, "the glory won by the Trojans shines brightest of all; for they died defending their homeland." [*Trojan Women*,386-387] As for the cleverness of the Greeks, which accomplished for them their victory and which remains in daily use by them to defend their ongoing atrocities, it is only a satin veneer over their barbarism.

Women, slaves, barbarians - all those designated as a race apart, so as to be marked for oppression or slaughter - are disclosed in their common humanity, even as the inhumanity of their masters and executioners is revealed. The lesson learned late and hard by Admetus - that every human life is equally precious and that the seemingly superior scale of his life and his concerns is a function of his proximity to them - simply pervades Euripidean drama. It comes down to this, as the frenzied Phrygian slave in the *Orestes* [1523] so simply states it: "Everyone likes to live... slaves too!" The same slave, an unlikely seer by any usual measure, points to the foundational truth for the political order, as it ought to be, when he says that: "Everywhere, anyone who knows anything at all knows that living is sweeter than dying." [1509] A truism to be sure; but like many truisms it contains a profound truth, neglected not because it is obvious but because its demands would change the world.

CONCLUSION

Whether noticeably or not, I have endeavored to maintain a certain critical distance from Euripides and his work in the course of this discussion.   Critical distance is not, however, the same thing as detachment, for which I have admittedly little capacity or patience. Seeing, hearing, and thinking - the most straightforward ways of approaching Euripides - are inevitably modes of engagement; and whatever insight occurs is the fruit not the foe of engagement. Doubtlessly, one human being may approach another as an object of study, as one might approach a rock in geology or a wasp in entemology or a star in astronomy; but I question the appropriateness and the fruitfulness of approaching an author in such a manner. Authors write because they have something to say; and we waste their time and ours if we are not as concerned as they that communication should occur. I am neither so uninformed nor psychic as to claim that the complexities of communication across centuries and between cultures are easily or ever fully resolved; but my instincts tell me that to foresake the heart of Euripidean drama to analyze its husk is more fittingly seen as stalling than as scholarship.

Admittedly, there is more doubt and dispute over the existence and location of a heart in a dramatic corpus than in a human corpus. Nonetheless, once the search begins, its pulse may be felt even in its extremeties and the heart traced from there. First, however, we must be convinced of the fact of life. Some translations, critical studies, and theatrical productions of Euripidean drama regretably fail to evince that fact. They display Euripides' work as if it were a fossil left long ago by something once alive rather than as something still alive and as capable as ever of leaving its mark. Digging up Euripidean drama, whether on a

149

stage or in one's study, is not to be compared with unearthing a fossil; instead, it is more like digging inadvertantly into a buried electrical cable. Once we strike it, we are convinced of its power; for, assuming we are grounded, we conduct it.

What is discovered in that moment of truth, when nothing any longer insulates us from the power of Euripidean theatre, is that Euripides, like Aeschylus and Sophocles, and perhaps like all great art, brings us back not to some remote site in times and places past but back to a center and a source always only an insight away. So much that calls itself theatre today derives whatever force it has from its own devices and resembles an internally combustive contraption able to turn a few tin wheels for our amusement and distraction. It was the genius and the courage of the Greeks, by contrast, to go out with a key and a kite, as it were, and to conduct storms.

Euripides, even more than Aeschylus and Sophocles, I believe, speaks with peculiar directness and immediacy to us today. His times were singularly darkened and confused, as ours are. The flight of the gods, the destruction of the earth, and the standardization of man - the marks of our times, in Heidegger's formulation - might as well have described Athens and the Greek world in the late fifth century. The ancient characterization of Euripides, however, as a playwright who wrote about people as they are and not as they ought to be could not in the end be less accurate. True enough, Euripides cast a mercilessly revealing light upon human cruelty and banality; but he also left us with heroes and with a vision of how we ought to live. If his heroes seem not to be such and if his vision seems to cast no appreciable light, it may be that our eyes are not yet accomodated to the darkness of our times, as Euripides' were to the darkness of his. In fact, his heroes have little in common with the archaic daimons of an earlier age or with the Christian saints of a later age. The heroes of Greek legend and literature, like the saints of Christendom, transcend death and thus are frequently ambiguous or compromised in their commitment to life. Euripides' low-brow heroes are more lucid and limited. The earth is their only utopia. They find themselves inspired by the vision of **a** future, without any ambition to envision or to construct **the** future. They live closer to nature than to history, history being the realm of delusion and violence. Like the Phrygian slave in the *Orestes*, they find the taste of life sweetest of all and assume that others do as well. Their heroism consists in living out the implications of that assumption. It is enough if they do nothing to add

150

to the suffering in the world. And, if this does not suffice for heroism, then so much the worse for heroism.

It is surely a sign of their confusion and perhaps their weakness that Euripides' characters change their minds as often as they do, an activity unfitting and unfamiliar to the heroes of an age more sure of itself; but it is also a sign of their thoughtfulness. Second thoughts, after all, can be redeeming as well as damning; and certainty is as dangerous as it is reassuring. Scruples, self-examination, and doubt may not make one singularly effectual; but at the very least they render one more or less harmless. Those who are unsure of themselves make less likely executioners or martyrs; and a world without both would be not perfect but would be an improvement.

Euripidean drama is not devoid of certainties and truths, however. There is the certainty of death and the sweetness of life. There is the beauty of human solidarity and the ugliness of its violation. There is right and there is wrong, however unclear one may be at any given moment regarding the face of each. This unclarity, after all, yields to clarity now and then. "Shameful is shameful everywhere." [*Andromache*,144] Racism, slavery, sexism, inequality, the violence which they breed and the violence which sustains them, as well as civil wars and wars of aggression: there is little doubt that Euripides found all of these to be shameful wherever and whenever they exist, now as much as then.

Finally, there is friendship, the bond of love, the bond between all mortals of good will. This is a friendship rooted in common suffering and committed not to proliferate it, yet nonetheless resiliently capable of forgiveness when we do. Both in his plays and in the following fragment [902] ascribed to him, Euripides seeks and offers just such friendship:

> The good and decent man,
>   even if he lives in some distant place,
>   and even though I never set eyes on him,
>   I count as a friend.